CRITICAL WRITING: STORIES AS PHENOMENA

Jamie Dela Cruz, EdD

Savant Books and Publications
Honolulu, HI, USA
2020

Published in the USA by Savant Books and Publications
2630 Kapiolani Blvd #1601
Honolulu, HI 96826
http://www.savantbooksandpublications.com

Printed in the USA

Edited by Eleonor Gardner
Cover by Daniel S. Janik

Copyright 2018 Jamie Dela Cruz. All rights reserved. No part of this work may be reproduced without the prior written permission of the author.

13 digit ISBN/EAN: 978-0-9994633-2-1

All names, characters, places and incidents are fictitious or used fictitiously. Any resemblance to actual persons, living or dead, and any places or events is purely coincidental.

First Edition: January 2020
Library of Congress Control Number: 2019953739

Dedication

There are many people to thank for the making of this book, but I would especially like to dedicate this book to my parents. To my mom and my late dad: Thank you for always being there to support in all of my endeavors, and standing by my decisions to take my career in so many directions. You taught me the meaning of unconditional love, and raised me to be the person I am today. You helped me have confidence in myself, and to do my best in whatever I attempt.

Acknowledgements

There are so many people who I would love to thank for helping me write this book. I do not think that I would have been able to accomplish such a feat without so many great people entering my life. These people have been a source of inspiration for me to do my very best and to strive for even the highest stars in the sky.

To my family, you have been the rock that has kept me sane. To my mom, thank you for all of your love and support throughout my educational and professional career. You have always made sure that I made good decisions in life and that I strived to be the best version of myself. You have been a great source of inspiration for me as a person and the way that I treat others. To my brother and sister, thanks for putting up with me and for your constant encouragement as I continued my studies as a doctoral candidate and now an author. You helped to build my confidence, especially when I did not know where my journey would take me.

I would also like to thank my dear friend and program chair, Zachary Oliver. Words cannot express how much I appreciate and value your guidance and words of wisdom. Thanks for always planting that seed in my head to always strive to be the best in what I do and for continuing to support me even when I was a little reluctant to try new things. This book would certainly not be possible without you and all of your hard work to get me started.

A special thanks also goes out to Michelle Harada for helping me throughout this entire process. She was there to assist me while completing my dissertation and served as my guide for helping me to recall the different experiences about my dissertation that you will read about in this book. It wasn't an easy journey to interview myself and through your help, my understanding of my experiences have become so much clearer; I certainly couldn't have painted such a great picture of all of my experiences without your help. Thank you so much.

Finally, I would like to thank my dissertation chair, Carol Parrington. You have stayed by my side from the beginning of my doctoral program and have believed in me and what I could do. You have helped pave the way for me to grow not only as a professional in my field, but as an individual as well. Thanks for all the support and encouragement over the years; it has really meant a lot to me.

Even when I didn't believe that I could do it, these people helped me to push through the hard times and to finally come up with my final publication that you are about read. I really am so thankful that these people have come into my life and have helped to shape my life. I can't thank all of you enough for your words of kindness, support, and of course, the great times that we have shared together.

Table of Contents

Forewords	1
Preface	9
Introduction	11
How This Book is Organized	12
Using This Book	12
Background Information of My Study	13
Chapter 1 - Phenomenology	17
Lessons Learned	28
Chapter 2 – Be Comfortable with Your Write Up	31
The Hard Truth	39
Lessons Learned	43
Chapter 3 – Understanding Interviews	45
The Truth	51
Lessons Learned	57
Chapter 4 – Setting Up Your Interviews	59
The Hard Truth	66
Lessons Learned	70
Suggested Checklist for Interviews	71
Chapter 5 – You Can Never be Too Prepared	73
The Truth	81
Lessons Learned	84
Chapter 6 – Build in Incentives	87
The Hard Truth	95
Lessons Learned	99

Chapter 7 – Seek Balanace and Prioritize Goals	101
The Hard Truth	109
Lessons Learned	112
Chapter 8 – Don't Rush or Make Assumptions	115
The Truth	124
Lessons Learned	129
Chapter 9 - Owning Your Dissertation	131
The Truth	141
Lessons Learned	144
Chapter 10 – Defending the Dissertation	145
Lessons Learned	153
Chapter 11 – Reflection: The Dissertation is Just the Beginning	155
The Truth	165
Lessons Learned	168
Parting Statement	171
Index	177
About the Author	205

Critical Writing: Stories as Phenomena

Forewords

"We shall not cease from exploration,
And the end of all our exploring
Will be to arrive where we started
And know the place for the first time."

— T.S. Eliot

Storytelling has a rich tradition in Hawaii that's experienced through music, dance, and the spoken word. The spirit of Aloha transcends time. T.S. Eliot and his quote shared in with this passage have woven in and out of my life to an extraordinary extent. On my own research journey, I have learned the timeless lesson of the lifelong learner: never cease your exploration of learning and researching. I love what I do, and I consider it a blessing, as my dear Hawaiian sister, Carolyn Darling reminds me whenever there is a passing shower.

I spent five exuberant years with my *O'hana* before we were transferred to Colorado, and then, to London, England for another Air Force tour. But, I knew I would come back to this special island, one day. After I finished my doctorate at the University of Denver, I returned to the islands, first for a week, then two, then three, crying every time we had to leave. In time, we happily returned to our island home, spending every winter, to the present day. I started teaching research and education courses, at Argosy University, Hawaii, on Bishop St. in downtown Honolulu where I first met Zachary Oliver, a dissertation student, now a great friend and colleague and mentor to all on qualitative heuristic inquiry. It was the same year that I met Jamie Dela Cruz. Jamie was in a few of my doctoral classes and was working on a dissertation about Aloha ʻĀina, an original Hawaiian curriculum based on the values, beliefs, and language of the Hawaiian culture, through oral history or, storytelling.

The curriculum and Jamie's dissertation were about experiential learning. The outcomes showed that students were able to connect learning through their exploration of the native Hawaiian culture and their natural environment. Jamie's dissertation used phenomenological inquiry, focus groups and interviews with teachers of the new curriculum. Phenomenological research is a holistic process, where authors must bracket bias and most importantly, realize the value of knowing oneself first, before even possibly relating to someone or capturing another's lived experience.

I have helped dozens of students with their dissertation research and observed their growth as writers and researchers. I investigated storytelling as a powerful methodology while working on my research project with a good friend and author, Carolyn Mears, who created a highly-effective method of storytelling, that uses an oral history interviewing technique captured in her book, *Interviewing for Education and Social Science Research: The Gateway Approach.* Carolyn's work and approach to interviewing was used to interview the parents and students from the Columbine High School shootings and to and collect data on their experiences before and after the event. While she developed the technique further, I investigated the backdrop of violence in society and schools, and researched character development. Unlike simplistic interviews, storytelling involves effort and risk, for both the storyteller and the audience. Storytelling is dynamic and changes the storyteller and the audience just from the act of telling stories. This ancient and devalued art is slowly diminishing, however, with the onset of newer technologies every day. It is the phenomena, or the story that is the heartbeat of the interview in phenomenological research.

I learned much from my own dissertation advisor and professor of qualitative research at the University of Denver whose teachings today impact my role as professor and dissertation advisor. One of my most memorable courses I took while attending the University of Denver was about interviewing skills. Most university courses cover this skill in one class or one day within the qualitative research course itself and thus, little is actually known or practiced by the student researcher before entering into the participant's space. One cannot begin to see through this glass darkly, before basic levels of communication skills are achieved. The interview necessitates a trusting relationship between the interviewee and the interviewer. Careful interviewing and meticulous analysis is necessary to gain insight into the phenomena. As such, the first step is to have no assumptions of the experiences of the participants, in advance. It is a phenomenally different paradigm then quantitative research! And, the researcher realizes, one does not arrive at the phenomena itself, but through analysis of the narrative, starting again, at the very beginning, the researcher arrives at the place where he began, as Eliot asserts.

In phenomenological research, the literature review is last, not first. As researchers, we have a responsibility to the participants, ethically and professionally, to interpret and edit the words and the stories related during the interviews and focus groups with care and sensitivity. Often this sensitivity is lost in the hurry to get the dissertation finished or to meet the (Institutional Review Board) IRB deadlines. Credit is due to Jamie, for his effective technique and member checks and rechecks in this arduous process.

Advice for other students might include a few ground rules: There will never be a perfect time, or enough time to work on your research. This is probably the most important lesson imposed when having other tasks, job, family *et cetera*, at the same time. Ironically, Jamie managed to accomplish far more research development while having a full-time job than other students who had more free time to work on their dissertations. There will always be roadblocks along the way that make it difficult, but do not surrender. There are different strokes for different folks as the saying goes, so you have to find your own strategy. Some students work a little bit on their dissertation every single day.

Jamie: "Sometimes while teaching, you just have to concentrate on teaching. You can't expect to work on a dissertation during finals' week." Time management skills are essential. He had to make some tough choices, but he never forgot the key to finishing: remembering that your research is important, will follow you for the rest of your life; that you are the expert on your topic, *pau*. Momentum is imperative.

There are those students, like Jamie, who hold a special place in my memory. Against many odds, whether it be personal, academic or professional, their desire to succeed and surpass their goals, is realized. They were not only listening…an important skill in interviewing and interpersonal communication, they could actually see the end game, and they did not give up where others did; they had goals, where others did not, they had passion, where others would not, they kept moving forward, each time they were knocked back; they took on difficult board-feedback and achieved greatness. Being in the academic milieu, makes you judge your self-worth by the standards that surround you. Momentum is imperative in this process.

Both my teaching career and research have made me reflect upon what makes a good professor, teacher and advisor. Although, I do not underestimate the importance of a highly developed skill base and a theoretical and philosophical understanding to inform the student's critical thinking ability. I remember Jamie was an extraordinarily bright and eager researcher, student, now good friend, and colleague. He still has a passion for helping children learn. I have always been interested in educating adults and youth with new and innovative ways of knowing, and have come to the conclusion that it is the "person" of the researcher, his own perception of reality and interpretation of the phenomena; that is not so much about what we do, as much as who we are at any given moment, in time. Students come to know who they are, how they perceive the world around them with purposeful work and their passion. It is in truth, a phenomena.

C.A. Parrington, Ph.D.

College of Education

Argosy University, Hawaii

I believe that there are people who come into our lives for many different reasons. In our lifetime, we meet many people who help us along our journey called life, and we keep those who are most important close to our hearts. This can be true for many people we meet as each one of us is very unique in the strengths that we bring. Without the support of one another, life itself would be very difficult to manage.

In my career as a student in the field of education, I have been lucky to cross paths with many influential individuals. This was most evident during my doctoral program where I was able to meet a colleague at

Punahou School named Jamie Dela Cruz, a student who had just completed a program in Organizational Leadership. He was a knowledgeable young fellow who also completed his doctoral degree at the same university that I was attending.

In speaking with Jamie, I was able to learn so much from him especially in terms of getting my study accepted by the Internal Review Board (IRB). For me, I was at a point where I was ready to discontinue the doctoral program because I had been attempting to successfully complete the process for a period of six months. Jamie's guidance really helped me through the process of making sure I was sensitive to the IRB requirements in order to properly gain approval, so my study could be conducted without compromising the overarching goals of my intended research.

Jamie was instrumental in making sure that I knew exactly what the process would look like and was able to clearly articulate the lay of the land to ensure that I would be able to continue my study. He spent countless hours with me at work, on the phone, and in passing to ensure that I would know exactly when my deadlines would be, understand what the board was looking for, while holding a continued interest in my topic to ensure that I would complete my study to the best of my abilities.

As he publishes this first book, *Critical Writing: Stories as Phenomena* (Savant 2020), I am honored to wish him the best of luck in his future endeavors. With his support, I have learned a great deal about myself and the ability to never surrender to seemingly insurmountable obstacles especially when surrounded by friends who provide unconditional support. Please enjoy his book and I am sure that you will learn immensely from what he has to share with you.

Kent Shanks

Doctorate in Business Administration

Critical Writing: Stories as Phenomena

Preface

The process of completing a dissertation was a little traumatic for me and discouraged me from any form of further post-doctoral writing for the longest time, swearing never to do it again. However, here I am again trying to write a book for all of you to learn from the lessons of my experiences from my dissertation. Thank goodness I never gave up! But after a year and half of rest and enjoyment, I felt that the time was right to share my story to help others who may experience the same type of frustration that I did. I hope that, through learning about my experience, you are comforted to know that you are not alone, and that others in your field have gone through the same feelings of anxiety at different points in their dissertation.

I am lucky to have an Ed.D from Argosy University, a Master's in Elementary Education and a Bachelor's degree in Marketing. In my career, I have been an elementary school teacher for more than 10 years, have taught at the University of Phoenix in their College of Education Program for the past 7 years, have organized professional development courses for the University of Phoenix in math, and served as an external consultant, grant writer, and program evaluator for companies here in Hawaii.

At Argosy University, there is now a support group that meets once a month to help support students who may be having trouble navigating themselves through the doctoral program itself or the dissertation process. At each meeting, the members try to invite different speakers to talk about their experiences in the program and offer words of advice to help students who are struggling in the program. I am honored to have been invited to one of these meetings and it was great to share some of the ideas in this book with those in attendance. Some of my chapters have even come from different questions that were raised by these students.

Sincerely,

Jamie Dela Cruz, Ed.D.

Critical Writing: Stories as Phenomena

Introduction

This book was created to help budding phenomenological researchers build effective research projects by learning from the mistakes of others. Just like any other study, no study is perfect. Each of us have made some mistakes that may not have been detrimental to the overall success of the research project, but, presents teachable moments for all researchers. In this book, I happily share some of those stories with you with lessons to be learned from each situation.

In understanding that no research project is perfect, we must strive to do many things well. Some of us may not be the best at all aspects of the research project, however, we must try to find ways to better ourselves in the way that we conduct research studies. As researchers, we should continuously look for our personal best and continue to do things at the highest level. Consistent focus on the important factors will make you shine as a researcher, and you will find success in creating excellent studies in your field.

How This Book is Organized

This book is designed as a series of lessons to help you organize your phenomenological dissertation and key points that I have never forgotten as a researcher. I believe that these elements and important concepts are vital in making sure that you set yourself up for a successful study. These lessons have been learned through real-world experiences and can help budding researchers apply these ideas in a disciplined way.

The title of each chapter in this book is a snapshot of a lesson learned. To introduce each chapter, I explain how this lesson was learned in the context of my own dissertation and the reasons why each is important. I then show how the lesson can be applied to your own dissertation and potential hazards or positive experiences that can result from each. The end of each chapter provides questions and/or ideas that you can use to help you as you move on with your particular study.

Using This Book

There are many ways to use this book and to apply the information in it to your individual situation. You might decide that this may be a book to read as you are going through your dissertation to make sure everything is in check. You may also decide to use this book to raise your own performance level and take your existing work or project to the next level. Alternatively, this may simply be a book that you may need as a source of inspiration to keep your drive for continued research going. However you choose to use this book, it is important that you put these lessons into your daily practice to improve your research. It will come down to ensuring that you are committed and consistent in making sure that you are your very best each day.

I wish you all the best as you read and apply these lessons into your daily routine.

Background Information of My Study

My study used a phenomenological approach to understand the perceptions of teachers who have implemented the *Aloha ʻĀina* culture-based curriculum in their classes within the context of one elementary school in Hawaii. The study involved group and individual interviews with teachers who were trained to use the culture-based curriculum in their classrooms. Efforts were made to build an open communication line with each narrator. I explained to each participant about the phenomenological "talk story" process of telling one's story in implementing the *Aloha ʻĀina* curriculum in their classrooms.

The *Aloha ʻĀina* curriculum is a culture-based learning program that enables students to learn about the many aspects of their local Hawaiian community. Within this program, there are curriculum units that are mapped out for students in grades three to twelve that cover different environments and Hawaiian practices. For this study, teachers in grades three to five who were using the wetlands, *ahupuaʻa*, and stream life units in their classrooms were interviewed. The *Aloha ʻĀina* learning units enhance student learning with a culturally relevant curriculum to inspire them to embrace *aloha 'āina* (love of the land) as a way of life. The *Aloha 'Āina* curriculum fosters place-based education strategies and integrates Hawaiian culture, terminology, and core values.

"Talk story" in the context of Hawaii is a relaxed term for carrying out a casual conversation among friends. This term was used to allow participating teachers to freely share their ideas as if they were in a conversation with friends and were open to sharing their true feelings without the fear of being judged or critiqued by an evaluator. In doing so, it helped the participants understand that I was there to support their experiences and not judge them for their successes or failures teaching the curriculum unit.

The study used a purposeful sampling strategy. The purposeful sampling of the study required that all teachers be certified to teach elementary students, be over the age of twenty-one, and that all teachers in the sampling implement the place-based curriculum in their classrooms during the period of at least one semester. The study included eight primary school teachers in grades three to five, who had recent experiences using culture-based curriculum.

This study used participant focus-group interviews and semi-structured individual interviews as the method for data collection. Once the participants met the criteria for participation, a focus-group interview and a follow-up face-to-face interview was arranged. The focus-group interview was completed in the school library while the second individual interview was completed in each teacher's classroom with only the participating teacher and I present.

Both the group and individual interview sessions were voice recorded. Participants' reflections were properly transcribed to ensure accurate documentation. As the individual interviews were scheduled, participants were asked to clarify previous transcriptions and were allowed to make changes as necessary.

During the debriefing in both group and individual settings, teachers reflected on their experiences using the curriculum and were able to ask additional questions, if they had any, and were able to add any information that may not have been adequately covered. This additional debriefing step opened new doors for success and attempted to make the participating teachers feel that they were as much a part of the study as the researcher was. These narrators then became partners in a journey that is critical in understanding phenomenological studies.

This study focused on understanding the lived experiences of teachers using culture-based curriculum within one site. To capture this story, the researcher used a multiple face-to-face interview design to provide the necessary contextual basis for adequate interpretation. The first interview was used to establish the context of the participants' experience. The second interview allowed participants to reconstruct the details of their experience within the context of occurrence. By setting up two face-to face interviews with all eight participating teachers, it allowed me to properly make sense of what was being said by the teachers and clarify meanings with their narrators on the subsequent interview.

To help give a clear picture of their experiences, I conducted two interviews, one interview during the beginning of the implementation process and one when they completed the curriculum units. The first interview was a focus-group interview with all the participating teachers helping to facilitate ideas and comments about the curriculum, which in turn helped me develop additional questions to guide the follow-up individual interviews. I also reviewed the school's accreditation plan and demographics to help validate recurring patterns and themes that emerged from the interviews and to check for any evidence of outlying data.

Chapter 1 - Phenomenology

Phenomenology allows researchers to see things from the perspective of different people. Phenomenology differs from different types of research strategies in that it calls for people to discuss their experiences of phenomenon to help others learn from their experiences. When conducting phenomenological studies, the researcher is asking for another's story and what this person thinks is significant and meaningful. Therefore, accurate stories are important. Also important, is for participants to disclose any pertinent information that needs to be shared with the researcher in order for the researcher to create a thick, detailed report of the true phenomena. Information within this context could include, but are not limited to, their experiences but also their feelings and emotions felt as they were going through these experiences. This could include anything that they remember in particular—either positive or negative—which really transformed their understanding or memory of this real phenomenon in their lives. Using my study as an example, it could be the joy of learning that a student or a group of students had exponential growth while participating in culture-based activities through the hands-on style of learning that was otherwise not heard of in their traditional teaching practices. This style of data collection is like telling a story from the perspective of different people. Storytelling and story-hearing offer a meeting ground for deepened connection, clearer understanding, and mutual learning. These stories help others to learn from insider information of others so that those who have not lived the experience can better understand what has happened.

Phenomenological studies search for a deeper understanding and description of everyday experiences that focus on the lived experiences of people. Through the use of interviews, phenomenology has a stressed importance on retrospective reflection of what participants have experienced and invites participants to share their stories in their own ways through guided discovery and semi-structured questioning. This approach allows the researcher to gain a deeper understanding of the perceptions of participants through careful questioning. Through this style of methodology, participants can share what they want to know and have learned as well as are able to add a dimension to our understanding of the situation that cannot be revealed through a questionnaire.

Humans relate to one another on many different levels, such as emotional, social, physical, and philosophical. Through interviews and conversations, the human experience and the significance that people take from their lives are taken in different ways; what one may take from the same experience can differ from one individual to the next. It is important that as researchers, we understand that we are gaining access to the perceptions of people while not analyzing those perceptions to say that there is only one correct way to understand an experience. The goal of phenomenology is to bring together a number of differing views. The goal also includes combining views to create a holistic picture of a particular event or phenomena. Phenomenology offers a creative means of connection so that the researcher, the narrator, and the reader all expand their understanding of a particular paradox of emotional perceptions and answers.

In the Hawaiian local culture, people refer to this style of speaking as, "talk story." Talk story is a means by which people share stories and culture. Like the phenomenological approach, talking story in a local and cultural setting allows people to share their stories in a very unobtrusive manner where people freely share their opinions through everyday conversations and important traditions and practices passed on to others. This style of data collection offers a cultural grounding for deepened connection, clearer understanding, appreciation, and mutual learning.

Stories to Hawaiian people, and many other ethnicities, are the staple of time-honored traditions and values that they hold true. The tradition of storytelling once brought ancient people together toward keeping cultural and family traditions strong. It is important to remember that not long ago, people from around the world were sharing their stories through storytelling because there was no means for written communication; talk story and storytelling sessions were the only way in which important beliefs were passed on from one generation to the next.

It is through the nature of these ancient practices that we have allowed powerful stories to be with us today. Although the practice of sharing these stories around a firepit would seem questionable, the nature of these practices is unquestioned. People have learned to appreciate the significance and meaning from these expressions of tradition and helps others who may not come from that background to better understand their practices on a resonant level where outcomes be better understood.

Stories today do not follow many of the same traditions that were once used in the past due to an increase in technology and advancements in living conditions. Despite this cultural shift caused by technology, some means of storytelling has been diminished and many stories have been well-documented and written down so that others can learn from them. Similar to phenomenological studies, the goal of storytelling is to learn from the experiences of the past, whether it be cultural or personal, to bring about change when change is necessary.

The reasoning behind why I wanted to name my dissertation "Talk Story" is, when we talk with our friends and family, we feel comfortable sharing things about our lives that we may not always share with strangers. People feel that when they enter conversations with familiar individuals that are trustworthy, the things that they share will be taken to heart and honest opinions will be shared. From there, more meaningful conversations about life, love and play stem and people learn to enjoy the opinions of others in a very relaxed setting whereby people do not feel that they are being evaluated and interviewed, but rather that they are able to share stories about their lives so that others can learn. Whether it be positive stories of success or of the mistakes that they have made, we have learned more about the world outside of our experiences through the stories of others.

Stories can come in different forms. Stories can be about the past, present or even the future. And through these stories we are able to learn about the world around us and make sense of things that we have heard about. For example, we may not have given birth to a baby or understand the pain and exhaustion that can occur as a result of child birth, but we may have some idea of what it may look like and the pain that a woman does encounter during the process. But unless we have gone through the experience ourselves, we have no idea of what the experience may *really* be like. As a male, I will never have the chance to experience this phenomena, but through hearing stories about it, I am able to appreciate the agony that a woman has to endure to have a child and to have empathy for a woman in that situation.

Like any other situation or experience, it is always good to expand our understanding of the world around us to become more empathetic for others and the situation that they may be in. Developing empathy and situational understanding allows us to prepare for events that could affect us in our own lives. From these understandings, we can better understand the context in which things happen and the conditions that cause certain behaviors and beliefs that people hold true because of their life experiences.

When using interviews in phenomenological studies, the interviewer is at the mercy of the narrator, while trust and relationships are at the heart of interviewing success. It is important that participants are comfortable with the researcher and the researcher's style of conversation. The researcher should create an environment that simulates general conversation, as if "talking story" is occurring with them. It is important to remember that the participants are the key to research and that only they can open the doors toward understanding their experiences. The participants' perspectives and responses are the heart of research given their ability to articulate their stories.

As the researcher takes the journey with participants, it is important to remember that the researcher and participants are partners in learning experiences. In many other types of research models, some participants are viewed as subjects and merely people who are supplying data for evaluation. However, phenomenological studies consider participants as people who are on the same level and are equals to the researcher. This research model in most cases is mutually beneficial to both the researcher and the participants whereby both sides are learning about the same experience.

Understanding this, we as researchers need to make the best use of the short time we have with our participants, and make sure that we listen carefully and hear their stories. I put an emphasis on this because in the whole scheme of things, you do not have a lot of time with your participants in order to get all relevant information from them. Time moves very quickly. Also, much time is needed for participants to recollect their understanding of a particular event and to also recall all of the intimate details that a researcher would want to obtain from them.

If a researcher tries to rush participants, participants may not have the appropriate time to make sense of their experiences. This may cause the researcher to overlook important aspects that may benefit from further exploration. In some cases, some participants may need a day or two to better articulate what they want to share with the researcher. It is important that the researcher provide an opportunity for participants to review and add to their transcriptions upon the completion of transcribing their interviews. Then, the participants can see how their responses may have fit with interview questions. When participants have time to better understand how their responses have properly answered the interview questions, they can sit down and better evaluate their experiences.

Like an interview, some people are pressured to find responses and sometimes blank out because of the high-pressure of the situation. We as researchers must understand that some people may not always feel comfortable being probed for their understanding of a particular experience, especially if the experience was not positive for them. Because of this, it is important to give participants time to understand the interview questions and allow enough time for them to respond. In doing so, participants have time to recall their experiences and are able to better understand their experiences through the interviewer's questioning.

As in the case of any other person, we don't know the exact situation of every person we are interviewing. Some people may have more on their plate than others. Some people may have appointments or meetings preoccupying them so that their mind may not fully be on the interview at the time. All of these factors can play a big role in the amount of effort that participants offer during the interview. As researchers, we must find ways to work with these people to obtain the most accurate data possible. Although we may not be able to dismiss inconsistencies created by "bad days" altogether, there may be some participants who may need more refocusing and probing to ensure that they are able to share an accurate representation of their experiences.

When doing qualitative research, it is important to keep in mind that there are no stupid responses or questions. What may be interpreted as stupid or irrelevant can close many doors for many researchers if they are not able to understand what participants are trying to convey in their responses. In many cases, participants are trying to evaluate and make sense of their experiences as the researcher questions them within the interview. Sometimes, this can be hard for some people to articulate as they try to fit interview questions into their understanding of what actually happened. Learn to be patient with participants during this process.

To me, the hardest aspect of conducting phenomenological interviews is probing people who have a hard time verbally explaining themselves or interviewing people who are not conversational. Sometimes, what may be the case is that some people do not enjoy engaging in meaningful conversation. Those who prefer not to converse provide responses that are "bare minimum" even if the researcher is prepared. With these types of participants, the researcher may go through the interviews relatively quickly, and may require asking more questions to get a better idea of the participants' overall experience.

In some cases, some participants may have blocked themselves from their negative experiences; some participants try to block out experiences that may not be as positive as they would have wanted for the circumstance. The majority of people remember mostly what they want to remember from a particular experience. In some cases, some participants may not be ignoring interview questions or refusing to answer them, but may not have remembered their responses as well as they may have wanted to remember their experiences. For these participants, it may take a little longer for their stories to unfold as they try to recall their experiences on the spot. When experiences are mentally blocked out, experiences may not be as vivid as they want them to be, requiring more time to make meaning from what they experienced and to really understand what they went though. In this case, it may take a little more time and may require the researcher to find different ways to probe participants for a better understanding without swaying them to say whether the experience was positive or not.

Although we try to find people who are "story worthy" many times our participants have a hard time articulating their experiences on the spot.

As researchers, we need to understand that sometimes there are people who are better at explaining their experiences on paper. However, some people are better at being interviewed in general, while some excel visually. Although phenomenological studies are mostly based on oral communication, some participants may need more help in explaining their thoughts. Some people may need examples of student work in front of them. Some may need to be in the environment that they were in when they experienced the phenomenon. Some participants may be able to explain their thoughts without any help. Be responsive to the needs of your participants and allow them to use things that are available so that they can be as expressive about their experiences as possible.

To aid in this process, it is also important to make sure that as the researcher, you are ready with good questions and are prepared for the unexpected. For me, I believe that it was important to think about my questions before going into an interview. Also thinking about possible responses that could come up and how best to deal with certain situations was important to me. Sometimes you can see how some questions could lead to different tangents, therefore it's invaluable to think about how you might refocus your interview into ways that can be most meaningful for your participants and for your data collection.

Although you may want to see where some of these discussions may lead, there are areas where discussion may not prove to be very valuable. This is important because you don't want your interviews to last a couple of hours with each participant. For these purposes, and for those who can be "too story worthy," it is important that you understand which questions are most important and where you may want to put more focus in order to prioritize your interview time.

The big thing to remember when doing phenomenological studies, is that we are purely there to appreciate their understanding of their experience. We are not there to evaluate them on what kind of people they may be or what kinds of predispositions that they may have, but merely to help guide them in their understanding and to help them properly express their feelings. Their stories alone will help to serve as the basis for your study. Also important is to truly understand their perceptions of experiences in order to fully analyze the current situation. This is a hard task to accomplish; it is a common tendency to evaluate others because their thinking is different from ours. Through conversations, it is vital that we keep an open mind and appreciate a different point of understanding and consider things from another person's perspective. Although these perspectives may not run parallel to our own thinking, it allows us to better understand others and their behaviors.

Through this experience from interviewing, we ourselves are learning how to allow others to learn from the same experience in the same manner that we have. We are, in a sense trying to best understand the participant's experiences in order to make better sense of how the experience fits into our overall understanding of the world. Through the narratives that we have learned about, a researcher's job is to properly articulate these noteworthy stories that help others to better learn about themselves through the experiences of participants.

Although this may be hard to take, we must allow our participants to become specialists in their field and allow them to do the talking. I believe that in order do good a great job, we need to take a step back to truly hear stories and to help clarify any areas of misunderstanding or areas that may not be clear with the participants by using semi-structured interviews; such a practice helps to guide discussion while not overtaking it. Our job is to help guide participants in ways that they can formulate meaning from their experiences, making sure that they can create a learning experience from it.

From personal experience, the phenomenological research model can be a fun one that can be very rewarding to both the researcher and participant. Enjoy your time during your interviews and take time to learn something different from each person. Each interview will be a new experience that should be treasured; each day is another chance to learn from others.

Lessons Learned

1. Phenomenology is the study of understanding people's lived experiences.
2. Each person can present a new learning opportunity and we must give them enough time to recollect their experiences.
3. Phenomenological studies offer a chance for mutual learning for both the participant and the researcher.

4. When conducting the study, remember that you are there to appreciate the story of your participants; you are not there to evaluate them individually or personally.

Jamie Dela Cruz

Chapter 2 - Be Comfortable with Your Write Up

After I collected and transcribed the data from both of my interviews, I reviewed the data carefully for underlying themes. A way to manage my assumptions and biases from what I had heard during the interviews, was to re-read my notes. This process of organizing and analyzing portions of the data was challenging because completing this task took many hours.

I initially thought that the write up and analysis were going to be easy and that my dissertation was going to wrap-up soon after I completed all of my interviews. From my experience, the data analysis of doing qualitative studies can be quite grueling especially when reviewing interview transcriptions; looking over large amounts of data can be quite frustrating and trying to make sense of everyone's answers can be quite challenging, especially when all of the responses are not aligned with one another.

For my dissertation, I had one focus-group interview and one individual interview with each of the teachers for about an hour each session. This amounted to approximately nine hours of interviews and roughly 70 to 80 pages worth of responses. Trying to manage this much data into four or five themes can be a very overwhelming task to do. It can take much time to organize the responses in a way that you can handle, especially when the transcriptions result in different tangents. The data collected within each question can also overlap with other interview questions. For me, most of the themes that arose had some overlap, while other themes were not clearly identifiable. It took many days and nights to organize the themes into bigger themes that would encompass the different responses, while trying to hone them in to ones that were manageable. Once I thought I had something going, I started writing down notes to help me to make the best sense of what my thinking was, to assist me in my write up and how I was going to present my analysis and findings.

As I started to organize my data, I started to make charts of each question that I wanted to ask and started putting down the different responses that related to each question on each sheet. When I was done with the responses that clearly fit into an appropriate category, I started to play around with the other responses to find emerging themes that I did not initially think about at first, but that started to emerge as I started to break apart each interview. As you can see, some of the themes will emerge quite quickly but some of the others can be more challenging to find, especially when you find some outliers in the data that can throw you for a spin. During any data collection method, you will have outliers; try to work with the responses and you may find that they are either not related to your study or may spring you for inspiration for a new theme that other responses, may in fact, validate.

In my dissertation, the teachers liked the utility of the curriculum, but there were certain sections that proved to be harder to analyze than others. In many cases, I wanted others to look at the data to verify that I was on the right track, and to see if they saw the same patterns of data that I saw. As the sole researcher, it is very important that you have more insight into the interviews because you were there to witness the participants tell their lived experiences and the intricacies of how they explained themselves. What I truly didn't want to happen was that I would misrepresent the data that I collected, and my participants would think that I didn't understand the point of view they were trying to convey to me. This is why I cannot stress enough the importance of taking notes during your interviews to really help you better understand the point of view of the participant. These notes explain the different behaviors the participants displayed when you spoke about uncomfortable situations or true happiness when they explained their successes. Notes can also help you recall and explain these behaviors that you may have forgotten about as you review the many transcriptions and interviews during your study. Notes will help you to best understand participant responses as you review your transcriptions and ways to help them better communicate their responses to you as you continue your interview.

The one thing that I was thankful I did, was to allow all participants to look over their interview transcriptions and make changes that they saw necessary before analyzing their responses. In addition to this, I also allowed participants to look over the analysis before I submitted my dissertation for final approval to ensure that they validated the same themes. With this safety net in place, I felt a little more confident that I would be able to accurately represent my participating teachers who I worked with, and they could trust that I was able to represent them in the best way possible.

Despite this, there were some uncertainties during the process, and I did second-guess myself in my evaluation of the process. For me, some of the overall themes were not apparent at first; I did have to look over the data repeatedly. In some cases, I did have a hard time articulating their responses in a way that really satisfied my liking, and I did understand that my committee did not have the time to look over all data to ensure that my analysis was done well. To help alleviate their stresses I spent a little more time making sure that I was comfortable with some of the overall themes before we had discussions about where to go with the rest of the data.

There were days that I literally went crazy trying to make sense of the collected data and trying to decide where I wanted to go with the given responses. I would just sit there for hours each day, trying to work with the data to find themes that I was comfortable presenting to my committee, which could paint an accurate picture to an outsider who may not know of have experience with the curriculum and experiences that I was studying. Everything that I was seeing really seemed to go back to three themes that

I originally formulated before I started putting all of my data together. Day after day, it seemed like Groundhog Day seeing the same information and not being able to step outside of the box to find new themes.

After some thought, I decided that I needed to give myself time off from organizing data to clear my mind of everything that was going on; it seemed as though I was going nowhere with the data and it was time to separate myself from what I was seeing in order to come back with a new and fresh perspective. After taking time, it really helped me to see the data in a new light and I was able to formulate different meanings from the same data that I had seen just days before. Like your dissertation, it is sometimes hard to see the faults in your own work when you see it too often. Sometimes it may take a day or two off for you to separate yourself from the current situation and be able to think more clearly, while remaining more focused on the participant's perspective rather than your own.

I was able to learn more about the data, and felt more comfortable knowing and understanding how my participants may have felt instead of bringing more of my feelings into the data. From this experience, I was able to better understand the lived experiences of my participants and from there, I was able to seek the help of my dissertational committee to help me formulate more focused themes that built on my understanding of the data that was in front of me. With this support, it helped me to make better connections between the data as I moved on to working on my conclusions in chapter 5. I was lucky that my dissertation committee consisted of evaluators who knew the subject well, and although they could not see my data, they were very good in helping me to make sense of the data that I was seeing. To this day, those discussions have really inspired me to really look outside the box and to really take time to understand data before making any conclusions. Without their help, I do not think that my dissertation would have been as successful as it was, and many of my conclusions were only touching the surface of the overall understanding of their experiences.

The one thing that I did have on my side was that I knew my data well, and I was able to articulate the responses to the participants. I explained my thinking to them and we were able to come up with themes that were most relevant to my study and the field of education. As budding researchers, I think that the terminology that we use are sometimes out of context and we do need some help in explaining ourselves, especially when it comes to conducting an evaluative study such as mine. And it takes certain key words to really make our work stand out.

As a teacher myself, I understood that my participating teachers were busy people trying to ensure that their classrooms were taken care of first. I understood that they were willingly giving up their time to be interviewed; they voluntarily gave up articulation times and time after school to be interviewed, gave up time to review transcriptions, and also spent time to review my analysis. What I didn't want to happen was to waste any more of their time by writing up a careless analysis because I knew that they were going to review it.

Critical Writing: Stories as Phenomena

For me, it took a long time to do a final analysis for my dissertation because I didn't feel that comfortable with my write up for a couple of months. Although it took a long time and a lot of discussion with my committee members, I think that the teachers were happy with the final analysis, and many of them were satisfied with the way I was able to articulate their experiences with the curriculum for that year. Although it took some time for me to internalize the responses and time with my committee to articulate my ideas, it was well worth the time spent.

As stated, it also took a long time to make sure that the correct academic language was used and to make sure that I was completely comfortable with what I would present to Waialae Charter School, their administration, their teachers, and especially the Pacific American Foundation who wrote up the curriculum. Initially, it was difficult to find a way to present the data in a way that was both culturally responsive (because the curriculum was culture-based) and able to paint an accurate picture of what the teachers felt about the curriculum. For me, I wanted to paint an accurate picture of how this curriculum was accepted within the study group of one school and to help the teachers who participated in the study to celebrate the areas of success that they had while also acknowledging the shortcomings and areas for improvement as well. The reality of phenomenological studies are to not only show positive areas to make everyone involved happy, but to have a balanced approach and to show the negative impacts that are there.

Although it was hard to explain to the organization the downfalls of the curriculum, they were happy to understand that there were areas to improve on, as they continued their rollout of the curriculum throughout the state. They knew some of the shortfalls that were mentioned, and were surprised and excited to find new ways to make their curriculum more effective for teachers in the field. This is what makes phenomenological studies so valuable to both the researcher and the participants. There is always something to learn from each experience and from pointing out areas for improvement in an academic and constructive manner, whereby participants are able to better understand their overall experience and ways to improve themselves.

In the end, after finally submitting my final dissertation, I understood that in conducting phenomenological studies, you do not need to satisfy the needs of anyone. Phenomenological studies are built to properly convey the experiences of people and do not serve as a evaluation of anyone. As I started to write up the analysis, I found myself trying to write up an evaluation of the situation when in turn my study only served to understand the experiences that these teachers had with the curriculum. Take time to understand the data in your study and always feel comfortable with your write up before moving on. Understand that it is ok to talk to other professionals in the field to help you make sense of your data and present it in ways that are most effective, in a way that suits your style and needs.

The Hard Truth

When all is said and done, you need to feel comfortable with your findings, and your overall study. It is important to make sure that you have carefully reviewed your data in order to make effective conclusions. You may not come up with the conclusions that you initially thought would materialize, but remember that the purpose of dissertations focused on phemenology, is to simply share the stories of others so others can appreciate and learn from their experiences.

When using a phenomenological approach, it is important to emphasize that you are not there to please anyone or to produce a report of how effective or great something was. You are simply there to make an unbiased review of a phenomenon that occurred. You become the expert and are there to help others understand what your participants have experienced in order for participants to learn from their successes and mistakes. There are always two sides of a study and it is important to present a balanced perspective and not only report on the positive aspects of the experiences.

Like everything else, there will be bumps in the road and you take each day as it comes. There will be days that you will begin to see new themes emerge and there will also be days where you are banging your head against the wall trying to see things from a different angle. Be patient and do not rush your study. With time, your study will come along, but I advise you to not rush and make ill-advised conclusions that could jeopardize the reliability and validity of your study.

If you need a software program to help you classify your data, there are some that are available. Some of the more popular programs include, Nvivo and Atlas. These programs can be quite helpful for organizing and analyzing data to help find themes before beginning to make analyses and conclusions. If you do have the money, these programs can help you save valuable time by organizing your data and setting up graphs.

I tried to use Nvivo at first, but it was a little hard to get my themes organized in ways that really made sense for me. I am not saying that it is not a great program, but for my needs, it really did not fit my liking. I like to see things visually mapped out; having it on a screen and on a small scale really restricted how I wanted to move my data around physically.

To me, I really appreciated having the opportunity to move my data using Post-It notes and being able to clump that data in different ways. Although the Nvivo program got me off to a great start by helping me to initially materialize some themes, there were some themes that I did have a hard time articulating and I needed to find a way to organize my data in different ways so I could better understand it. As I organized them in different ways new themes formulated in the process and I was able to find meaningful discoveries in the responses that I was reviewing. For new researchers, it may be a one-stop shop to help you organize your data depending on what kind of phenomenological study you may be doing. Conversely, for others, like me, it may be a great starting point to begin from.

In many cases, you may find yourself lost in the piles of pages of transcriptions and it is ok to feel frustrated. When reviewing your transcriptions, it is completely normal to feel overwhelmed, but it is important to keep focused and to be patient with your data. You are not going to be able to write a phenomenological analysis in one day or a week after collecting all of your data and it is important to make sure that you take time to know your data well. This will definitely help you in case you need to seek the help from your committee members who are not going to review all of the transcriptions, to help you write your analysis and conclusions.

In some cases, it was hard to see certain themes arise and for me it was sometimes beneficial to get away from the data. And when I came back to review it again, some of the responses seemed to make more sense to me. When you see the same set of data over and over again, everything sometimes seems like a blur and they all seem to fit under the same category no matter how much you look at it. You may want to give yourself some time off to make sure that you are able to separate yourself from the data from time to time, and come back to the data with new and fresh ideas on where to take it. This can remove yourself from the fixation that you may have had on certain themes and new ones may arise once you start looking at other studies or even reviewing other parts of your dissertation.

Once you have organized your data, it is important to make sure that you are able to clearly express your findings. Some of the technicalities will come in word usage, specific terminology, or even formatting the presentation to show that you are knowledgeable in your field. Very important is to internalize these important factors because it can go a long way in showing others how seriously you take your work. Others may also notice the sophistication of your work and really be impressed by the work quality that you are able to produce.

In conclusion, it is important to make sure that you take the time to know your data before presenting ill-advised conclusions. You may need to take some time to organize your data into ways that are most meaningful to you. For me it was important to look at the data from different points of views and organizing it in different ways before I could really understand what was in front of me. I did, however, suffer through a lot of headaches and stress doing it the way that I did, and I wish that I was able to understand the importance of separating oneself from the data, long before I realized it. By separating yourself, it offers you an opportunity to have a fresh start to seeing different things from a different perspective if only you give yourself some extra time to do it correctly.

What was important was that I was able to put aside all of my assumptions of the curriculum, so I was able to present a well-balanced approach to the overall analysis which shared the experiences of the teachers in the study. Although this may be hard to do, because we all have our own dispositions and preconceptions about certain things. With help, I was able to come up with conclusions that really helped to share the stories of my participants that helped to increase curriculum development for all of the stakeholders in the company. This effort did however, take some guidance and a lot of extra practice, it was eventually done well, and

I was very pleased with the results.

Lessons Learned

1. Be patient with your data.
2. Look at the data from different points of view.
3. If you need to use software programs, they are available.
4. Put aside your own assumptions.
5. Share *their* stories.
6. Be comfortable with your findings.

Jamie Dela Cruz

Chapter 3 - Understanding Interviews

Interpersonal communication skills are needed to communicate with another person or with society as a whole. Through these communication skills people are able to formulate their understanding of the world and to make sense of why people act and behave the way that they do. This is only done through people who share their thoughts, ideas, and experiences with another through verbal, kinesthetic, and written processes. These communication channels allow us to better understand other people and their behaviors. In doing phenomenological studies, it is important that we understand the importance of good interpersonal skills because our research is so involved in effective communication with others.

In understanding this, it is vital to have good interpersonal skills when doing phenomenological studies. As the sole research tool, you must be an effective communicator to make the process successful. No matter what, you will be required to talk to and work with others in a way that will require great skill. If you are unable to clearly communicate your goals and questions with your participants, you will never be able to get the kinds of meaningful discussions that allow you to understand the true experience that your participants partook in.

To aid in this process, it is important that researchers use language that is appropriate for their target audience in order for participants to make the best response that they can. Sometimes, we as researchers, try to use highly technical words that can make questioning our participants difficult because they do not completely understand what is needed from them. In order to best help participants with questioning, it is important to keep in mind that we should all be able to use language that anyone can understand. As you develop your set of questions, keep in mind that they should sound like "everyday conversational questions" (i.e. general conversations) to keep the mood of the conversation very relaxed.

One important aspect of phenomenological studies is to understand that our participants are allowing us into their world of experiences. We are, in a sense, a guest in their world of reality; it's important to know since they are the gatekeepers of knowledge for this study. For example, if they are not comfortable sharing information with you, they can give you all the information you may want to hear but may not let you in on the true realities of their experiences. This is where many researchers can fall victim, as they try to rush to get the data they want and do not allow new discussions to develop, which can open many doors for successful new discovery of their experiences.

Sometimes as researchers we try to evaluate participant responses and validate what we think is true about the overall experiences. This big mistake, can happen as you go along with your research. Our job as phenomenological researchers is to learn from the experiences of our participants and not judge their response, or to confirm our own preconceptions about the situation but to appreciate the experiences that these subjects have had.

As in the case of my dissertation, I saw myself falling into this situation. As I started to interview my teachers, they talked about all the great experiences that they had with the culture-based curriculum. I was in awe of how well the curriculum was accepted on campus. I attended the training sessions that many of these teachers went to. Although I was a little overwhelmed by the complexity of teaching such curriculum, I was so impressed by the enthusiasm that the teachers all showed in the beginning of their initial focus-group interview. Many of the teachers were so happy with the curriculum and the utility of it that they used it to supplement ongoing campus efforts of making their curricula more hands-on.

In writing up my reflection notes during the interview, I too felt rejuvenated by the responses that I got from my questions; that I was in this amazing situation where all of these teachers had only positive experiences with this curriculum unit. I continued my questioning by talking to the participants about the different components of the program and the different experiences that they had and almost all of the responses were very positive. As I continued, I started to probe for more of these positive experiences, as no one really spoke about their negative experiences with the program. The initial interview seemed to have ended with great success. The teachers and I were both happy with the outcome of the first interview.

As I started to analyze the data, it seemed like an ideal situation whereby teachers were so happy about the curriculum, they didn't seem to have any trouble in implementing the curriculum in their classrooms. That was great news for me, as I heard so many great stories of how effective this curriculum was in helping Native Hawaiian students. This seemed like it was going to be such a great project, and I was going to come back to the curriculum writers and tell them about all the positive things that the teachers had to say about their curriculum.

Compared to my program evaluations and phenomenological books, my situation felt so unique, like something was certainly awkward about the whole situation. Never before had I heard about interviewing going so smoothly, and it left me wondering why in the world had write up a consent sheet indicating that the interviews "may bring about feelings of anxiety" and all of that nonsense. My first interview went so great that almost all of the teachers had only good things to say about their experiences, and they were all so excited to start articulating with one another so they could see what the other grade levels were doing. In addition, they all felt so great about using the curriculum in their classrooms.

As I started to write follow-up questions for the post interview, I continued to write more follow-up questions on fabulous success stories that these teachers had to share. This is where I was cautioned by my committee to try to follow-up on some of the little things that I may have overlooked. There were some comments made about the teaching of the Hawaiian culture that came up, but nothing that I thought was important at the time. Much of what I heard about the curriculum seemed to be so positive and it seemed too good to be true.

In review of the entire situation, I now understand the power of the snowball effect that can happen in focus-group interviews. As I asked my questions, many of the teachers did have positive things to say about the curriculum and as the conversations continued many more people added on to their positive comments. This snowball effect allowed the conversation to move in one direction, and everyone started adding in their positive comments. Whether the participants understood what was happening or not, the conversations moved itself into different tangents of a similar positive experience. I can't say for sure why this happened. One speculation could be that that the teachers were trying to tell me what they wanted to hear because they thought that I was a representative of the company. Another speculation could have been that no one initially wanted to speak out against the positive experiences of the group as they would appear less credible or that they were less experienced in front of their peers.

As I continued my interviews with the participants individually, I learned that all of them suffered from different struggles with the curriculum and all of their experiences were not successful as I initially thought from initial focus-group interviews. Without that guidance, I could now see myself going along and not truly understanding the struggles that I saw teachers falling into when I was first introduced to the curriculum.

Throughout my dissertation, I had many different opinions about the curriculum and the experiences that I hoped to see come forth from the study. In reflection, I believe that although it is good to have my own opinions on the conclusions before I started, good researchers need to put those assumptions to the side and allow the research to grow naturally and not try to validate what you think is true. As I started my interviews I thought everything was so great only to find out that many people struggled with the curriculum in their own and unique ways.

It is important to understand that as phenomenological researchers, you are not there to confirm what you have heard about different things or to create assumptions about anything. You are there to simply learn from their experiences. It is important that researchers understand their role in doing phenomenological case studies, and that researchers are there to support their participants through seeing things from their point of view and be able to articulate it in ways that others can learn from.

As hard as it may be, there are perceived levels of power that exist within each relationship. For example, when a child is building a relationship with a stranger. The child initially views the stranger as someone who cannot be trusted. In the researcher/participant relationship, sometimes people may view you as another researcher who may try to take advantage of their responses and misrepresent their responses. The key is to understand your role and how your participants may react to you and find ways to open the doors of communication through building strong rapport, either through small talk or proper explanation of your methodology.

In-depth interviewing is no different from having purposeful conversations that are created as a form of social dialogue. At first, the conversations are more of mutual sharing and then builds into more purposeful communication whereby information begins to unfold and the researcher can then begin to learn about the experiences of the participant. Only when the participant is ready to allow the researcher into his or her experiences will these meaningful conversations begin to move along. Thus, do not underestimate the power of initial impressions.

As you continue with your conversations, it is important to clearly show to your participants your genuine interest so they will allow you into their world. The hardest aspect to understand is that in this relationship, the participant has all the power. They have the ability to share as much as they want with you and they also have the ability to keep everything important from you as well. Unlike the teacher-student relationship, you as the researcher are at the mercy of the participant and you need to do all that you can to build this relationship to get what you want.

The Truth

Interviewing is the hardest part of doing phenomenological studies because it requires a lot of skills. These skills could include, creating meaningful relationships with your participants; reading participant reactions and understanding their needs; being able to probe participants to better understand their experiences; or even finding ways to have them best articulate their understandings. As the researcher, it is important that you are able to collect both reliable and valid data throughout your study because there are so many external factors that could affect the analysis and conclusions once you are done with your interviews.

As phenomenological researchers we need to understand that although we do have needs to get our data, our participants also have needs as well. Participants need to know that they have a safe environment to share their experiences and a trusting relationship with the researcher that they can depend on. The stories that they share with us can evolve from these basic, yet significant opening discussions. Through establishing rapport, further conversations will reveal the experiences that each individual understands to be significant depending on their overall understanding of the situation. In order for the participants to bring about and reveal these experiences to you will depend on their comfort level that they have with you and how well you can bond with them.

To help build this kind of rapport, it is important to make sure that you build an environment of trust and honesty. If you are able to build a relationship where participants see that you care about their feelings and are there to support them in their efforts to bring about their experiences of success and failures, it will definitely go a long way in helping them open up to you. Sometimes, it's more about the discussions that happen outside the audio taping than the ones you have on tape. In understanding this, it would be beneficial that researchers begin with small talk before beginning to record your participants and start drilling them with your set questions. In this manner you can help to build some type of connection with the participants and to help them understand that you are interested in their lives and well-being and not just your interview.

Like a child meeting a stranger, they will generally not tell researchers their life story unless they have some kind of connection to them. Whether they start talking about themselves or if you try to get information from them, there needs to be some type of connection before people begin to trust others. This all starts with some type of physical, emotional, or even spiritual connection whereby the "child" understands that you are someone who can be trusted and therefore become willing to share a piece of their history with you. Once that initial contact is made, discussions that are more meaningful can be created as people become more familiar with one another and they learn to mutually learn from each other.

It is important to connect with your participants on a personal level in addition to the professional level that you will have with them. This will help show the participants that they are not just a subject to study and that you genuinely care for them and their well-being. Like the ideas of the social exchange theory, these relationships grow through increased satisfaction of self-interest and how their needs are being met. As you continue with the study it important to make sure to keep that sense of empathy for the participants and their feelings and respect their opinions whether you agree with them or not. If any clarification is needed, I have learned that it is important to restate your understanding of their explanation in ways that may make best sense to them in order for them to best understand their experience.

Although you want to make sure that you are there to understand their experiences, it is important to understand your role as a researcher. You are still a professional who is looking to understand their experiences and not a friend who is there to solve problems in their lives. While conducting your research it is important to remember that your relationship with participants must remain at a professional, academically-focused level, whereby they are able to contact you in case they do have any questions about the study, but not to be counselors in the overall scheme of life. I am not suggesting that you cannot create lifetime friendships once the study is over, but during the data collection period, it will make your life a lot easier if you keep your distance from your participants to keep any biases outside of your research.

In-depth interviewing can be an enlightening experience in both positive and negative ways because we never know where the conversation may take us once meaningful and intense discussions arise about a topic. If discussions bring about feelings of fear, anger, or bad experiences, it is important to foster these discussions in a positive way. It does take skill for the researcher to turn these experiences into a self-reflection period whereby participants can learn from their past and create social meaning from their experiences. As these discussions continue, you need to be able to think quickly and come up with new probing questions to help develop important conversations that may create new discussions that open up new avenues for further themes that can be followed up in subsequent interviews.

Be warned; do not let these conversations go downhill and create feelings of apprehension and anxiety, as you want these interviews to be a positive experience for you and your participants. You want your subjects to have some time to vent out their fears or disappointments about their experiences which may lead to more avenues that can be explored. However, you want to make sure that your participants are able to maintain good mental health. There is a point where you may want to further explore their thought process but there is also a point where enough is enough. Feel out your participants, as each person will be different. Some may be able to learn from their experience as they learn to better understand them and become able to reflect on the situation as a positive, learning one while others may just be very negative and fearful of the experience which would not be good for future interviews.

Sometimes participants venting out, may lead to conversations that go way off topic. This is sometimes okay to do as your participants may need time to clear their minds to later be focused on the task at hand. These off-task times can be very fruitful as it allows the participants to get what they want off of their chest and then they can better concentrate on your next questions. Never rush your participants to move on as this process does take time for them to create meaning from their recollections of a particular event. Sometimes your conversations may go off topic for a little while and if discussions do not eventually move back to the topic, you can help to guide them slowly back to other questions that you wanted to explore.

As you hear these conversations whether it be on topic or not, it is important to keep your preconceptions of them and the situation to yourself. You are the researcher and you are trying to learn from their experiences. It is very important to let the participants talk about and explore their experiences through your guidance and not share your perceptions. This will help to keep the participant focused on their experience and not be pressured to answer your questions in ways that will satisfy and confirm your ideas.

Researchers in phenomenology need to understand that you are the guest in this relationship and that you are asking to learn from others. These people have a breadth of experience that you and others want to learn from. Phenomenological studies allow people to learn from others' experiences. To best understand and learn from these experiences, it is important that you understand the lay of the land of what you are studying and allow the stories to come from your participants with proper guidance.

There is so much to learn about interviewing and the skills needed to be an effective data collector. As an aspiring researcher, it is important to learn from other researchers so that you do not make the same mistakes.

Although it may seem that there is so much to learn about and master, this is what makes doing phenomenological studies so exciting. Take time to enjoy yourself during your data collecting and make sure to really take time to appreciate the experiences of your participants.

Lessons Learned

1. Create a trusting relationship with your participants.
2. Remember that you are there to appreciate their experiences, not to evaluate.
3. Keep a relaxed interviewing environment.

Jamie Dela Cruz

Critical Writing: Stories as Phenomena

Chapter 4 - Setting Up Interviews

Setting up interviews can be a very tricky process because the following initial decisions that must be made: how many interviews you would like to have; when to conduct each interview; how long each interview should last; and what kind of structure to have within each interview. There are so many different facets of the interviewing process that are sometimes overlooked. Many of the research models will suggest using multiple face-to-face interviews to help you gain many opportunities to provide a solid base for fair interpretation. This will allow you to meet up with your participants in more than one occasion to ensure that you are able to follow up with any questionable responses that you received the first time around or to find new angles to approach your participants that were not explored during the initial interview. In other words, you are creating context for learning in the first interview, and the second interview is to help your participants reconstruct their experiences into a meaningful way within the context of which it happened.

For my study, I chose to use multiple interviews. When I looked at my study and the perceptions that I was trying to explore, I found it most beneficial to have a pre and post interview whereby participants would be interviewed once, before they started to teach the curriculum to see what kinds of previous experiences they had with using place-based educational strategies. My second interview would serve two purposes. The first purpose was to follow up with the first interview to clarify any questions I still had in mind about their responses and for them to clarify any responses that did not sit well with them or that they wanted to expand on after reviewing their first transcriptions. Secondly, it would be to understand their overall experiences in using the curriculum once they had completed teaching all of the units after a period of one quarter or nine weeks of school.

Some models will suggest using more than two interviews depending on the research model and the period by which you will be collecting data. For me, I chose a different path. After my findings, analysis and conclusions were completed, instead of interviewing my participants again, I presented my final two chapters with all of the participating teachers and the principal of the school. I went over all of the major points of my analysis and conclusions and asked if any of the participants felt that the sections misrepresented them in any way. Each participant was also given a copy of the final two chapters to verify that their responses were represented and analyzed in the most appropriate way.

In having the participants take part in the overall process and give input at each stage of the process, it gave them some ownership to their responses. It also allowed them to see that their lived experiences would help to improve the current curricula. When talking with the developers of the curriculum, it was important to them that the participants of this study feel empowered in understanding that their input would be taken seriously and by doing so, they could bring about positive changes within the curriculum's development. By taking the time to do so, it not only helped them better understand their role in the overall process, but also served as a means for reliability and validity within the study.

In using multiple interviews, the interviewer can spend some time getting a feel for each participant and the kinds of personalities that they have. In doing so, the researcher can spend some time during the first interview to open up communication channels and to create a rapport with each participant. In subsequent interviews, once a relationship has been established the researcher can ask more probing questions that will capture greater detail from the participants lived experiences.

For my first interview, I chose to do a focus-group interview because I expected the teachers to have different experiences in using place and culture-based strategies in the classroom. I understood that this school had already been using place-based strategies in their curricular units, but there were new teachers to the school who hadn't. By setting my interview up in this way, I was able to have the teachers who were more experienced in using these strategies, start conversations that were meaningful to them and to have the less experienced teachers learn and build on their discussions. It was hoped that through these types of discussions, the less experienced teachers could see the challenges ahead and to better understand how they may best approach teaching the lessons in their classrooms before they began the implementation process.

Focus-group interviews can—and I do mean can—be a very positive and a negative experience for participants. On a positive side, focus-group interviews can provide opportunities for participants to hear other peoples' responses before answering on their own. Focus-group interviews also provide participants a little more time to formulate their answers based on what others are saying. In doing so, they may be offered more opportunities for success and have a basis for understanding before they are asked to make sense of their own experiences. In doing so, participants are able to piece together what they have heard and try to fit those responses in with their own experiences to formulate meaning from that. This can be very helpful for bringing about potential ideas from participants who may have a hard time expressing themselves—ideas that they may not have thought of on their own—and for encouraging participation during an individual interview. On the flip side, it can be a negative experience because once these discussions keep going, they can snowball and get out of control. Sometimes participants may jump on the bandwagon of discussion and only add to the current discussion without truly thinking about their own experiences, even if their experiences were completely different. What we should be doing as phenomenological researchers, is to try to get our participants to understand their experiences so that positive change can come about. If they are only using previous responses as a means to think about their experiences at a surface level and are therefore not able to draw from their true experiences, we are not doing our job as researchers; nor are we effectively getting through to our participants. Herein lies a true challenge in doing this type of research.

For my second interview, I chose to do an individual interview to help my participants better articulate their responses in a "safer" environment. By doing this, I felt that the less experienced teachers could safely share more of their insecurities about the curriculum that they may not have wanted to share in front of the other teachers the first time around. I understood that being new to a school could initially be a little intimidating, and to admit all your faults and lack of experience could be even more daunting.

I chose to conduct the individual interviews with each teacher in their classrooms with all of their student work and/or student examples displayed. In doing so, I hoped that it would help the participants recall some of the positive and negative experiences that they had with the curriculum as I went through my interview questions. These "artifacts" did indeed come in handy as some participants would think about the different projects done in class and some would bring out examples of student work that they remembered as being meaningful to them and were able to better articulate their responses with concrete examples. In being able to see these projects, the teachers were able to talk about their experiences with detail that would not have been possible if we had conducted the interview the school's library.

Looking back, I believe that those small changes in environment that helped cue participants to bring about the most accurate recollection of their lived experiences, was critical to the success of my overall dissertation. By having concrete examples in front of them, people are able to better articulate their experiences in a much more thick and descriptive manner. In addition, being in the same environment that the experiences occurred in can also help to bring about better descriptions because it brings them back to the place where all of their experiences actually stemmed from. Although it can bring about positive or negative responses, it is beneficial to do so and is critical to the overall success of your dissertation.

In addition, it is important to bring a watch or a clock to each interview. Before setting up your interviews, it is important to inform your participants of the approximate timeframe that they will be asked to participate in. Although we cannot give a definitive time span for interviewing because each person's ability to articulate their responses is different, it is important to give them a guideline by which they can prepare for. It is expected that in certain interviews we may not use the entire time or may even go a little over, but make sure to plan accordingly and allow for ample time to collect your data. And try to stick to those time limits to the best of your ability.

Also important in conducting phenomenological studies is the use of good interview questions. These questions will help you to properly guide your participants to understand their experiences and are critical to the success of your study. Although you will not be able to prepare all of the possible questions that you will ask in your interview, your set of interview questions should help you to address the overall research questions of your study and to help guide you in finding out the phenomena that you are after.

To help guide my focus-group interview and my individual interview, I used semi-structured questions that were open-ended and I also created follow-up questions. I understood that in each interview, there would be possibilities for new exploration that I could not prepare for. As a researcher of phenomenological studies, you do not want to restrict the scope of the narrator's responses, which may prevent you from discovering new terrain that you might not have anticipated. These tangents can and sometimes will, offer you new avenues for a better understanding of their experiences given that each participant's experience is different. I anticipated that as these tangents would arise, I would have the opportunity to ask more probing questions to understand the rich stories of each participant.

To me knowing the school and the types of curriculum that they were using were very important in helping me decide how best to structure my interviews. As I look back, I think that having this knowledge and doing homework on your participants can be very critical in the way that you approach your interviews. Although my interviews could have also been done well without knowing this information, it was easier for me to anticipate what kinds of discussions I would have so I could best prepare valid questions to the group.

Looking back at my research, I would suggest to all researchers that before doing any research that they find the time to know their participants to better understand how they can best help their participants in finding meaning from their experiences. Although you may not be able to access all of the information about participants, gather as much information as you can to best prepare you for the road ahead. It will sure make your life a lot easier.

Before closing up your study, it is important to allow your participants to discuss any other topics that they felt you did not touch upon. By doing so, it allows your participants to better understand their experiences in a way that is meaningful to them and to clarify any misunderstandings that they may have had. It is important that your participants are not limited by your perspective on the research study and that you are appreciative of any other topics that they may want to explore with you.

The Hard Truth

As you can see, there are many facets of setting up an interview that need to be kept in mind. This is not to say that the way that I structured my interviews is the only and best way to conduct a study but is a guide by which a research study can be done. For your research, you may not want to use a focus group and an individual interview like I did, but understand the advantages that each can bring and then pick the best choice given your study with consideration of the outcomes that you would want to get from each method.

In my experience, you will read many of the phenomenological research books that will explain the methodology to you but they never explain what the reasoning behind using such strategies are. In this chapter, I wanted to present to you the reasons why I chose to use the design that I used and the advantages that I found through using them; in doing so, it would allow other researchers to better understand alternative ways that they could fit in creating their own interviewing model of their own.

It may be hard to think about all of these things before you actually collect your data. And choosing your methodology and collection methods can be difficult enough. I would just suggest to researchers that although you may not know what to expect before beginning your actual study, keep these structures in mind and be mindful of your interview set-up to best help your participants bring the most accurate picture of their lived experience.

Being a dissertational student can be hard because in our program, we are restricted in our ability to collect real data. For some of us, this may be our first experience in working with this amount of data and collecting it in this fashion. In spite of this, we must be as prepared as we can be and be very mindful of our participants and the situations that we put them in to get the kinds of outcomes that we would want to get.

By using qualitative research like the phenomenological approach, we may use semi-structured interview questions with open-ended questions that help guide our interviews; it makes it difficult to know exactly where our interviews may lead us. The desired information that we want to capture may not be imminent and we may even open doors to feelings of anxiety, fear, or even anger. As much as we may want to stay away from these types of negative feelings, encountering anxiety, fear, or even anger during your research may be the only way to have participants better understand their experiences in a way that can be constructive for them. As researchers, we need to prepare ourselves for unexpected events and plan for strategies for dealing with potentially uncomfortable situations. This is exactly the challenge that we find in using qualitative structures. Although it may allow us different avenues for success, it can also put us in potentially difficult situations that can bring about negative feelings from our participants. This is why we need to prepare and understand the reasonings of why we choose to set up the study the way we do. As we already know, much of the research once it has started is out of our control and is in the hands of our participants. For many researchers this can be a difficult thing to deal with because we want to be in control of our research outcomes as much as possible. This is where we need to understand that we can only prepare ourselves for so many things in our interviews and there will be times that we ourselves need to move outside of our comfort zone in order to better understand the experiences of our participants.

In a sense, we become an outsider and move the power and knowledge-base to the participants in our study; the participants become the "experts" who we are learning from and need to use the knowledge-base of our methodology to guide them through their journey of recalling accurate descriptions of their overall experience. This is why it is so important to set up comfortable relationships with your participants where they are able to share their insecurities with you and together, you are able to create meaningful discussions that may not be obviously important to them. In looking back, I have learned that it is so important to offer your participants an opportunity to discuss areas that they feel are important and that they know that they are not restricted to examine areas that you feel are most important. In doing so, it creates an environment of empathy and one where they feel that their understanding of their experiences is held in upmost importance.

Taking the time to show your participants that you are interested in what they have to say can go a long way. Participant-researcher discussions can have the potential for opening a new world of discovery for others and continued research in your particular field. This is why these conversations should be discussed and lessons be learned from them. If you choose to do so, you can continue to engage in additional research after your dissertation that can offer other researchers a chance to consider further studies as they better understand your suggestions for further research within your study.

Qualitative research can be very difficult to conduct but can provide an excellent means for learning. Qualitative studies require more preparation on the side of the researcher in order to produce a quality study. Much of the study is based on value judgments that help capture what we may call "insider" information so that others may learn from their experiences. This approach allows researchers to capitalize on lived experiences in a way that brings life to qualitative academic research.

Our challenge is to extend our participant's personal experiences and relate those conclusions into the academic field. Many critics like to criticize qualitative studies for not having academic rigor because there is a lack of credibility because there is gray area when it comes to truths within the data. Through taking the time to set up our studies to be both reliable and valid, it gives so much more credit to the hard work that we do in qualitative research.

Lessons Learned

1. Take time to develop rapport with participants through a multiple-interview format.
2. Select your interview format with your participants in mind.
3. Have good guiding research questions to help you format your interview.
4. Be prepared for the "road less traveled." Unknown tangents should be explored.
5. Choose an interviewing environment that supports the process of recalling lived experiences.

Suggested Checklist for Interviews

Bring:

1. A good voice or video recorder that is able to record participant responses clearly. If you will be in a larger space while conducting interviews, you may need to bring a microphone.
2. Spare batteries in case of mechanical malfunction. Use fresh batteries at every recording.
3. An extra cassette or video tape in case the interview runs longer.
4. A copy of your interview questions.
5. Pens or pencils to take down notes.
6. Two copies of consent forms for each participant. One will be for them to sign and give back to the researcher and the other for their own records.
7. A journal to write down any notes or researcher biases during each interview.
8. (Optional) Snacks and/or refreshments to lighten up the mood for participants.
9. Wear appropriate attire. Dress for the occasion and know your audience.
10. A clock or phone to make sure you stick to your time limits.

Jamie Dela Cruz

Chapter 5 - Never Too Prepared

For my dissertation, I went into my individual interviews with set questions that I wanted to ask all of my participants during focus-group interviews. I was excited to start interviewing these people in order to learn from their experiences. I can remember being so excited to hear their stories and follow-up with my scripted questions that I had prepared for the interview. As I moved further along with my questions into descriptive questions about the curriculum, my discussions never came about, despite expecting these to materialize. The discussions that I sought to explore then snowballed into other unexpected tangents that were very intriguing to learn from but were not tied into my initial questions.

At first, I was a little thrown off by the somewhat sidebar conversations that I felt were not pertinent to the ideas that I was initially expecting. I wanted to explore these sidebar conservations as these seemed to be very important to the participants themselves and allowed the discussion to flow into new tangents of discussion. These conversations were indeed very positive interactions that allowed for further articulation between the teachers who came from different grade levels who did not completely understand what the others were teaching in their classrooms. From these discussions, the teachers were able to better understand reasons why some students came into their classes with the experiences that they did and how the teacher's lessons in the previous year better prepared their students for the lessons the following year.

These discussions led to other discussions about the potential overlap of material covered in the different grade levels and ways to make their coverage of material more efficient as they went into higher grade levels at the school. From these discussions, it allowed me to see the dynamics between the teachers and to better understand the experience levels that each teacher had. By doing this, it helped to make everyone more comfortable to share their ideas in ways that could be beneficial to everyone and not only for the researcher. It also allowed them to create a basis to recall some of their experiences from and to help them to bring about some experiences that I could follow up with as the interview continued.

For me, I did not know what was about to happen or how this discussion would continue, but it seemed to be a very meaningful to everyone at the table. In allowing them to explore different avenues of that they were interested in talking about, it offered me an opportunity to think about things that were important to these teachers and to find ways to further explore these tangents when I would meet with them in their individual interviews. During these discussions, teachers were able to ask their own questions that may have been lingering in their heads without my guidance and to allow for somewhat of a guided learning experience. They were able to bring about new avenues for continued conversation, which is a critical component of a successful phenomenological study.

As I listened to their conversations, I jotted down what was happening down very carefully in my notebook to take note of the comfort level, the story-telling ability, and the body language of each participant. As these conversations continued, I was surprised to see that as they continued in their articulation with the other teachers using the curriculum the participants maintained such a high respect for one another and their experiences through using the curriculum whether it be positive or negative ones. These dynamics are important to understand as I could see that despite not agreeing with the group, the participants were very accepting of their views and that the focus-group interview was a good choice to get discussions to build. From those notes, I was able to come up with new ideas that I wanted to follow up once the participants were done with their current discussion and I would have a chance to further guide their discussion.

As much as I wanted to guide this discussion and bring the participants back to my research questions, I needed to allow these participants to guide their own dialogue with one another and address questions that they too felt were important. Through having these conversations, it allows the participants to feel as though they are just as involved in their learning as I could be in such a situation. It was important, however, that the level of professionalism was kept at a high-level, and that people respected one another in order to enable the rich discussions within the group. Each person was cognizant of each other and the opinions that each had about the curriculum given their level of teaching experience in using place-based or culture-based curricula.

I can remember participants asking each other what was being taught in each of their individual grade levels as they tried to figure out how the curriculum spiraled and while exploring the overlap the curriculum had. These conversations were very important to the teachers who wanted to know how they could best implement their projects in their individual classrooms without overstepping in teaching. As a teacher myself, I was able to understand the importance that this discussion could have for their school as a whole. Although this was not something that interested me before I started the interview, I was able to see more of the different personalities and viewpoints among the group about the curriculum and whether or not they were excited about implementing the curriculum or not. Through these discussions, I was able to recognize which of the teachers was more comfortable implementing these culture-based lessons and which of the teachers were uncomfortable.

In some cases, I found myself trying to backtrack to determine the questions that were already being answered from the questions I had planned to ask, while deciding how to follow-up with some of the responses. It is always hard to make the decision to make a break in discussion because stifling the creativity of participants should be avoided when in the heat of such great dialogue; stopping such a dialogue could stop the flow of ideas. Deciding which parts of the discussion are important stopping points is such a key component of doing phenomenological studies. The researcher must be able to help facilitate rich conversations, which can be beneficial to both the researcher and the participants.

Sometimes, we can get so wound up in creating the perfect questions just to find out that those questions weren't as relevant as first thought. Although this can be a very frustrating aspect of the data collection process, it can be the most exciting, as you always want to be prepared for discussions with your participants. Never knowing what you may get once you start dialogue with participants is what I found to be so interesting and exhilarating about the whole experience. It is just like teaching; everyday is different and we can never be too prepared. Just when we think that we are as prepared as we can be, life throws us a curve ball where it is our job to find out how to make the best of it.

For me, I was only looking at the situation from my vantage point and created questions based on areas that I wanted to explore. I then tried to relate those questions to my overall research questions. Although this may have been a great start to preparing myself for the start of the interviewing process, I did underestimate the importance of being prepared for the extra tangents that were to occur. Although it was a very enlightening and great experience to see how different discussions could bring people to bring about different experiences depending on how they understood each question, it was difficult for me to allow these conversations to move in the direction they did. Looking back at my experience, I was so confident that the interviews would follow the flow of my questions. Although I wanted my participants to follow this flow, the discussions took me for a ride. As much as I wanted to move them back to fit my format, being flexible was the best thing I ever did. I allowed the participants to take off into their own direction and those discussions came out to be more productive than I could have ever imagined. The thick descriptions that they were built, helped me begin to see different themes emerge right before my very eyes.

This is not to say that if any sidebar conversations occur, not to stop them and let them keep going for as long as they want to, but take time to listen carefully to their responses and see if where your participants choose to go could be a productive avenue. Sometimes there will be times that we will need to end each discussion because they may start to turn into unproductive conversation and we do have to honor everyone's time. Remember that you do still need to get through your set of questions and other questions may also lead to more productive conversations that your participants may build on.

Although we want to worry about the little details and map out everything that we expect to happen, we always need to stay on our toes especially when dealing with phenomenological studies. You can be as prepared as you can in any situation. However, you should be geared up to go with the flow especially when discussions take a turn and new meaningful conversations begin to surface in the situation. You may never know what kinds of doors may open up for you and your study without trying too hard to guide your participants in ways according to your desired direction. In life, it's sometimes best not say anything but to let things happen while not worrying about where the situation may take you.

Therefore, in looking back, I think that it is important to set yourself up with a strong foundation of good research questions in the beginning; this is something that will help you to start on the right foot. In my experience, I wouldn't worry too much about the minute details. I also wouldn't have presumptions about where the discussions would lead. Please be assured that good things will happen as such was the case for me. Many times, people try to move ahead of themselves and want things to go in the direction of their interest. If things go in a different direction people become thrown off. If your dissertation is set up soundly from a methodological perspective and if you, as a researcher keep an open mind, you are truly setting yourself up for a great experience.

As odd as it may seem, we sometimes get so excited for things to happen and try to prepare ourselves so much for the event that we forget about some of the fundamental things that will help to make our lives a little easier when doing our study. These could include getting enough sleep, dressing appropriately for the situation, or even taking time to chat with your study participants to make them feel welcomed and not just a subject of your study. Please do not take these things lightly as these can really make a big difference in how people perceive you and your study.

As I look back on my experience, it was truly an experience that I will never forget as I tried to worry about every little thing. Once, I was so worried about making sure to have batteries for my tape recorder so I could capture all of their responses on tape, I forgot my dissertation notebook and my participant consent forms. Luckily, I had my flash drive with all of my files and was able to print them out before the interview. As much as we would like to laugh about these moments, they do happen. As human beings, we are very concrete about being prepared for a situation. Instead, we should take a step back and take things one step at a time.

When I look back I should have drafted a checklist of things to bring to the interview, reminder notes to keep myself on track, or even had a book to help me with my organizational skills. For many of us, we like being told what to do, making our lives so much easier. Being organized and ordered, gives us the structure that many of us crave. By being organized on your own and having a checklist or by having a guide to follow can really help to set yourself up for success.

It is important to know that understanding your study and your research questions is just as critical in setting up a great study as can the small things that we labor over too much. I believe that although the small things are important for setting yourself up for a successful interview, you also need to make sure that you take care of yourself. I also believe in ensuring that you are ready for the challenges ahead, which can go outside of the preparation that you have done before conducting your interviews.

The Truth

The dissertation process can be a very frustrating process of making sure all that of your "T's" are crossed and all of your "I's" are dotted. You really should make sure that you are ready for the challenges that are ahead, especially in doing qualitative research strategies because much is left to interpretation. In addition, questions from your committee can be used to come up with your research questions, interview questions, and analysis especially when they can never be quantified, like quantitative studies. It is imperative that you set yourself up with a good foundation from the beginning to ensure that you get yourself off on the right foot.

As you move along with in the dissertation process, there are mundane processes that could literally drive any sane person crazy. What I suggest to you is to stay on track and organize your chapters in a way that makes most sense to you. Although many experts will have their opinions of how to best write dissertations, I feel that when working with phenomenological studies, it all starts with a solid introduction and good research questions that will further guide you toward your goal.

For the first three chapters, it is important that you start with good research questions that will help to guide your study and what you want to explore. This healthy beginning will help you to stay afloat during the stressful aspects of the dissertation process. If these questions are truly based on what you are interested in learning, all the pieces of your dissertation will fall into place once the foundation pieces are put together.

From these questions, a literature review will become an easy component to put together. Based on what you will be working with and what you want to find out, you will need to create a foundation for continued learning that will help to build upon the current literature. This literature review will serve as a basis for current understanding that you will add to the context of your study, so it is important that you have a solid chapter of existing literature.

With this in mind, it is important to not get too ahead of yourself and piecemeal your dissertation together without solid research questions, which may take you a few weeks. In this time, you can map out different aspects of the case that you may want to explore for research. This can be a very exciting time for researchers as they try to talk themselves through the different scenarios that can happen and to think about ways to take their research. This is the time to make sure that you find something of which you are interested in learning. This effort will help to make your study more pleasant.

As ideas begin to materialize, it is important to understand that your research may not always follow a path that you expect of it. In phenomenological studies, the data can throw you a curve ball at any time, based on the responses of your participants. Although you don't want to exclude these outliers from the possibilities of outcomes, you want to make sure that you keep an open mind of what can happen. Take the time to really listen to your participants and allow them to sometimes create their own path for their own discovery. This discovery can unlock many new doors for further exploration once they are opened. In doing so it opens new opportunities for mutual learning.

Let the ideas flow from your rich discussions. Even if they do not match up with your research questions, you have to let the discussions continue in their own tangents at times. Although this can be a very time-consuming process, you may never know what other avenues you may need to explore and always know that you will have time to follow up. Whether through e-mails or through the review of transcriptions, you can always follow up with your participant. It is critical for you to write down your thoughts that go through your mind as your conversations happen. Doing such will make sure that you are able to clearly articulate each person's ideas. As you read through your transcriptions, you can allow your participants to further clarify their thoughts or to ask new questions that you may not have considered initially during the interview.

One of the biggest mistakes of a researcher is to be too closed-minded and to shut all doors for further success from opening. Although you may be happy with your results and see that your initial preconceptions of the study did come true, the learning and the experience of doing phenomenological studies are never realized in the truest sense. One important aspect of doing these kinds of studies is to explore the true feelings of you participants and for the subjects to self-reflect on the experience where they are able to critically analyze the experience and learn from it. They are then ready to tackle new problems that may arise while truly experiencing and understanding their positive experiences.

Like children who are so excited for the first day of school, researchers gather all of their school supplies together the night before school—or the study. As excited as they are to go to school, they sometimes forget that their shirts are backwards. Even worse, they forget to brush their teeth in getting ready for school. Wearing a shirt backwards and not brushing one's teeth would not be a good situation for making friends on the first day and not especially good for making a good impression as a good student for the teacher.

The lesson learned here is that it is important to be prepared for your study, but it is more important to make sure that you take time to enjoy the process. There are so many aspects of preparing for the interviewing process and I can see how some researchers can follow research models to a "T". No matter how prepared you may think you are, qualitative studies specifically phenomenological studies, can really take you for a ride. Like a trip with friends, being prepared, packed, and having a schedule can be great but life is always better when you take the time to enjoy the trip and sometimes do things that you never expected.

Lessons Learned

1. Start with good research questions.
2. Good questions can always lead you to new avenues for success.
3. Enjoy the ride of the phenomenological study.
4. Don't be THAT absent minded kid! Always keep a checklist of what you will need so you don't forget the necessities in

conducting a phenomenological study.

5. Make yourself a checklist to follow during your study.

Jamie Dela Cruz

Chapter 6 - Build in Incentives

I believe that the dissertation will be the hardest portion of your university program since it is the capstone project before you enter the work field and become an expert of your respective field. At times, I felt that the dissertation process was intensive and overwhelming. I eventually learned the importance to work at my own pace and to find ways to make myself feel that I was worthy of celebrations especially, when I completed different benchmarks in the program.

From my experience, there may be some who may need a little more encouragement than others while there may be some who may be able to work for longer periods of time without taking any breaks. In many cases, I have seen many students give up because the process can be frustrating and because they gave themselves unrealistic timelines to complete their dissertation, which of course does not always go as planned. For me, the waiting time for the Internal Review Board's review, final editing and publishing of the dissertation really took longer than expected and really got me flustered because in my head those processes should have been much shorter.

Despite setbacks, you will eventually get to the end but do anticipate that there may be bumps in the road where you may need to add a few months to your planned timeline to ensure that your work is properly published for others to read. As a doctoral student, I found the need to understand that my project could, and probably would, set me up for a future career and that it was best to make sure that I learned all that I could under the proper mentorship and great people to work with. So make sure to select your committee properly and make sure that you will be able to work effectively with those you select.

Throughout my dissertation, I found times when it was hard to continue working. Unlike what is experienced from working, the dissertation results in negative cash flow for you and never seems to give anything back until you are done, which is what I experienced. At times, it felt as if I was always walking up a never-ending mountain that kept getting steeper and steeper. However, I can assure that when you are done, the feeling is one that cannot be explained in words. You feel accomplished and complete when you are done. It does however, take some reminding throughout the journey that the journey is sure worth going through.

To help me get through hard times and maintain some sort of sanity throughout my dissertation, I built in my own incentives at each step. This can be hard to do because everyone wants to keep plowing through the final paper as fast as they can. For me, I took things one-step at a time and found ways to reward myself for my hard work. Whether it be through having a night out with friends, buying something that you have wanted, or even giving yourself a day of to relax, these little rewards can make a big difference in making sure that you stay on task and complete things in a timely manner, as I personally realized during my dissertation.

It has been said that with less time on your hands, people perform more efficiently. This can be true for many people because when we have less time we don't find more ways to fill our time with mindless and sometimes wasteful activity. This can be true during your dissertation phase as well. By giving yourself time to rest and enjoy yourself, you are able to focus more clearly on the bigger goal, which is to get through your dissertation. Like a battery, you need time to recharge to be at your best so that when you're required to step up to do a duty, you'll be able to perform at your ultimate level.

As I went through my dissertation, I found ways to make myself believe that I deserved these little incentives despite wanting to keep working through the hard times to make the process go faster. What I learned to understand is that this process does take time and usually lasts the average person a few years. Although we would like to make the time go faster, there is time within these few years to enjoy our lives. Although it can seem like a burden to take important time off from writing while wanting to keep focused, there will be times that you will need to take time off to enjoy the simple things in life.

Like work, going to school is like a fulltime job—it was for me. Although most people today manage to do both because of the cost of education, no person works 24 hours a day and seven days a week. My advice is to take some time off to spoil yourself and enjoy the fruits of your labor. Like work, our dissertation should be treated no differently. Finding time to go to work along with finishing school can be stressful, I recommend that you find a way to reward yourself for all of the hard work that you place in to your career. Without breaks, life would not be enjoyable.

For me, I love to shop and getting myself new things every now and then. When in the dissertation process, I found it hard to even get to a mall due to the time constraints with work and school. There were times when I wanted so badly to get myself a new phone or to just go out and get some new clothes to go out (even though it was hard to even go out) but in most occasions, I stayed at home to finish more work that I felt was more important. Although I did pay the price through health for the pure lack of sleep and constant work, I eventually made sure to set goals for myself and follow through in rewarding myself. Please make sure to follow through to occasionally reward yourself as your efforts will make the wait more than worth it! Given how arduous the process was for me, I celebrated with friends and family and made sure that the celebration was well worth the wait. Whether my reward was getting new clothes, having a nice weekend out with friends, getting a new iPod or even taking a short trip to visit family, I made sure that each celebration was celebrated to its fullest. Although some incentives were a little more costly than others, I always found ways to understand what made my clock tick to inspire me to get through each hurdle. As I understand this concept I would like to encourage all of you readers to celebrate the little accomplishments no matter how small these may seem. These efforts made a world of a difference! I recommend that all dissertation writers create some type of schedule of rewards.

The worst thing to do is to trick yourself into believing that you are going to have a reward set aside for yourself only to find out that after all of the hard work, you only work more. This strategy could really set yourself up for true burnout and the work will never seem to end. There needs to be some type of enjoyment and satisfaction after all of the hard work and your follow-through is very critical. These little celebrations can go a very far way in keeping you motivated to plow through the work and to see that there is a light at the end of the long tunnel that at times can seem so far away. The goal is to create mini goals within the bigger scope of the dissertation so getting to each benchmark doesn't seem so bad at all.

Through the dissertation process, there were different milestones that I strove to really set my sights on. The first milestone was the prospectus and creating of a committee; second was passing the Internal Review Board (IRB) and project approval; and the final being the final binding and publication of the dissertation. If you would like to keep the celebrations to the bare minimum I would choose these times because they mark the ending of one process and the start of the new as it was for me.

As I completed the previous step and I moved on to the next part that was built on the old. For me, these critical points in the dissertation were especially important. I made sure that the incentives were a little bigger to make sure that I would put together my best work the first time through. At the end of each of these milestones, I really honed down on what I needed to get done and stayed on task knowing that something good was in store for me. I did not give myself anything until I finished these chapters. I also made sure that no matter what, I promised myself I would make sure that I got it.

Funny as it may seem I am only now celebrating what I really wanted to do for my graduation present to myself, which was to take a small trip to the Mainland when I completed my doctoral program. Yes, from the time this was written, it has been a year and a half since I have completed the final binding of my dissertation. And I know that I said to follow through, but I am finally doing it for myself. In my defense, I did go on another trip to visit family who threw me a graduation party. And although it seems as if I celebrated graduating a lot with friends and family after I completed the program, the trip to the Mainland seems like the icing on the top of the cake as I try to finish my the publication of this book.

For me, one of the biggest hurdles for completing my dissertation was completing a proposal, especially putting together my methodology chapter and getting though the IRB (Internal Review Board). From my experience I became so frustrated with the first three chapters to the point

I wanted to pull out my hair and go crazy. This was especially true because my review board was not departmentalized by program, having different expectations of my proposal from individuals who were from different departments at the university. In my case, the board comprised of a doctor from the College of Education, member from the College of Psychology, and one from the College of Business. When reviewing dissertations, each college takes different approaches to the methodologies and data collection and when all members do not agree on your write up it can really make it more difficult to satisfy the needs of all committee members.

This process of getting your dissertation through the IRB can, and usually takes a few months to get through because of the technicalities of setting up your study. In this time, your IRB will carefully review your study to ensure you do not cause any harm to your participants during the interview process. In qualitative studies, we as researchers need to be cognizant of the well-being of participants. This is especially tricky using a phenomenological study because we can bring about different feelings of anxiety, fear, depression, or trauma which can have long-term effects on your subjects. Although it may take you a little while to refine your consent forms and ensure that your participants are safe during the interviewing process, the wait is sure worth it.

I am not saying to celebrate after completing each page that you write or to celebrate every week. However, find a balance in life and make sure that you find time to give yourself a pat on the back because it doesn't come very often.

The weeks before dissertation completion feel longer because you are no longer on an academic schedule and there is no schedule to tell you when each component of the dissertation is due. You are in a sense, your own internal motivator responsible for making things happen quickly. It is important to make sure that you are able to keep yourself inspired to continue your efforts toward completing your dissertation. Unlike any other time in your college career, a well-deserved pat on the back can't come at a better time to encourage you that everything will be alright while you're in in such a time of constant criticism and frustration. Yes, there is an end to all of the constant questioning and consistent, constructive feedback on your work. Your committee members are really there to help you become the best that you can possibly be.

Although my advice may be hard for some of you who are concerned about making ends meet, find ways to celebrate given the financial situation you are in. Some rewards can be free while some may cost you very little money. Regardless, find the time and necessary resources within your grasp as you can go crazy without these small rewards. These steps helped to make sure that I was motivated to keep working throughout the whole dissertation. There is no doubt that without these rewards, I would not have made it through the dissertation process as I found so many bumps in the road along what seemed like a process that would take a lifetime.

No matter what goals and rewards you set forth for yourself please make sure to follow through on your promises to yourself. So be cautioned to choose your goals carefully and pick ones that you can live with. Please do not go into major debt for the sake of being sane throughout your dissertation process because the cost of tuition for a doctoral program can be a major cost on its own. Pick rewards that you can afford given your lifestyle and your life will be so much easier and enjoyable.

The Hard Truth

Life is too short to be working every day and have nothing to look forward to. If I were to tell this statement to anyone who knows me well, they would laugh because I tend to drown myself in more work. Although I try to spread this mantra to the doctoral students at my university whom I encounter, it is a hard thing to enact upon concentrating on the task ahead. The thing to remember is no matter where you go or what you do, there will always be another wall to climb or another hurdle to jump. So, when does the list end? It never does. So when one accomplishment is complete, take time to celebrate it before you move on to the next and really enjoy it to the fullest; just like people who work full-time jobs enjoy celebrating and going out on the weekend after a tough week at work. They understand that after they put in a week of hard work, they will reward themselves with a night out or with having a few drinks with friends. It would only be possible to catch up with the millions of things that we have to do if we stayed at work 24 hours a day, every day of the year. However, we sometimes need to find that balance of doing work and having time for ourselves to "recharge our batteries." It is the same for people who are in the dissertation process. Yes, you could do more work on your dissertation by working one extra night and staying home instead of going out. However, there would be nothing to look forward to if all you did was work. Understand that the dissertation can wait until the next day and that a few hours of fun once in a while will serve you well to rejuvenate yourself. Like a job, there needs to be some down time in order for you to be ready to come back to the work and feel comfortable doing so.

This is not to say that this milestone plan is the only way for you to be successful but serves as a model by which you can adjust and schedule for yourself. You may need different incentives at different times that are not consistent with my suggestions and I believe that it is ok to do so. What I am suggesting is that you find ways to keep yourself motivated to continue the dissertational journey without burning out and to find ways to celebrate your mini accomplishments within the program as you see fit for yourself.

This concept hit closer to home for me when I was a junior in high school and my dad was diagnosed with pancreatic cancer. During his last six months of life since learning of his condition, his motto was, "celebrate every reason" to ensure that everyone who came to visit him understood that we should not take life for granted. My dad's motto helped people who he knew to take time out of their busy lives to make sure that they were thankful for what they had no matter how much or how little they had. Although in today's world everyone is trying to get ahead, make more money, and be more successful, all of those things cannot compare to a life full of happiness and enjoyment.

As in the case of my dissertation process, there were times that I felt defeated and that even though I knew I needed a break, I kept working in hopes of getting the dissertation done a lot quicker. What ended up happening was that I burnt out and was in such disgust with the overall progress of my final paper. In this time of repugnance, I took a couple of months off from writing. I loathed in my disgust of what was happening and decided that a plan was needed in order to keep my focus on the real goal at hand. I set up a schedule to reward myself for each milestone that I could see in the near future. I was able to break apart the final stages of my dissertation process starting with the passing of the IRB board and made sure that I was motivated to complete each part by setting up rewards that I knew would inspire me to do my best. In reflection, I believe that I should have set up this kind of system earlier in the dissertation process. It was not wise to keep working without incentives because as a student you can really get so distracted from the realities of what life is about when you see the road ahead of you. For me, I don't think that I would have made it through the dissertation process without this schedule and believe that this realization is what carried me to finish the program and become the doctor I am today.

In understanding these wise words that were passed on to me, I do understand that I need to live by these three simple words: celebrate every reason. Although it may be hard to do when money controls our lifestyle while there is no way around working, we must learn how to not only work hard but to find time to celebrate the things that we have done well not only for ourselves, but for others. Take time out of your busy day to look at things that you should be thankful for.

This style of living is what we should all strive for in life and should apply to our daily lives not only as a doctoral student but as adults in the work field. It is important to celebrate our achievements in life and to enjoy the fruits of our labor especially when it is well-deserved. Although this may be hard to implement in our lives because we are constrained by time, we must remind ourselves on a daily basis, to really take time out of our "busy" days to be thankful that we have things and learn to appreciate our loved ones who we are able to celebrate our accomplishments with. Our time on earth is too short to be stressed out each day and we must find a way to find a balance between work and play.

No matter where we are in life, life is a balancing act. Whether it be sharing it with someone special; spending time with your children, your immediate family; or finding time for yourself we must always have something to look forward to while having incentives for ourselves. Incentivizing accomplishments can really help keep us focused on our goals and accomplishments. This is the journey that we hold for ourselves and it is important that we learn to enjoy the journey of life we are on. Without goals, it would be very hard to appreciate life and the hard work that we do in our everyday lives.

Lessons Learned

1. Celebrate your accomplishments no matter how small.
2. Make sure to follow through on your promises to yourself.
3. Find a balance of work and play in your life.

Jamie Dela Cruz

Critical Writing: Stories as Phenomena

Chapter 7 - Seek Balance and Prioritize Goals

I still laugh to this day and tell this story to all of the people who ask me about my experiences in my doctorate degree program. When I first started my program and went to orientation, the facilitator talked to us about the demands of school and how much work we would have. During the orientation, I looked at the required course work and the classes that we were to encounter. The courses seemed general in the beginning and more focused in the specific degree as a student moved further into the program.

The facilitator explained that the doctorate programs were very intensive, and that the amount of time you would spend on coursework would be like having a full-time job. She insisted and made it a point to tell us that we should warn our friends and family that for the next couple of years we would be busy and that our time with them would be limited. As a social person, I laughed to myself because I swore that being overwhelmed by the program's workload would never happen to me, and that I would be so diligent in my work that I would certainly be able to continue to spend lots of time with my friends and family while still holding on to my daytime job.

When the program started, I continued to find time to meet up with friends on the weekends, occasionally go out to exercise and spend quality time with my family. Life was great! As the program continued, I decided to take more than six credits, which was necessary to become considered a "full-time" student. Increasing my credits would also mean that I could start my dissertation sooner than expected. When I increased my school load through extra credits, I found myself completely inundated by the workload. Each night and each weekend, I found myself swamped in school work and trying to keep "my head above water" in both my professional job and the workload from school.

As a budding elementary school teacher, I spent lots of time at school by going in early at 7 o'clock in the morning and not going home until 5 or 6 o'clock in the evening. It was a very hard time for me as I was trying to figure out the curriculum that we were using at the school, while making sure that I was ready to teach the material the next day. Upon arriving at home, it seemed like the two to three hours I focused on school work each night just wasn't enough. I was falling more and more behind in my work trying to be the best at work and in school.

After a while, something had to give. The following year, I decided that I wanted to focus more on my schooling so that I could finish in a timely manner. In order to do that, I had to reduce to a part-time job at my workplace, which allowed me to have more time to do well in my doctoral program. Although this was a little hard on me financially, it was well worth the sacrifice to get to my goal of graduating as soon as possible. I was able to complete all of my coursework in less than two years and spent two months completing my comprehensive exam.

It took me four years to complete my doctorate program and I spent two of those years completing my dissertation. Although this may seem quick to some, the last two years felt like it was an eternity at times. In some cases, I thought I would never get through the dissertation process, and that I would never graduate after finishing the coursework and comprehensive exam. It really was a tedious and grueling process that has been unmatched anywhere in my academic career.

In looking back at my experience, there were times where I was so overwhelmed by the whole process that I literally wanted to throw my paper in the trash and be over with it. When I looked at the early versions of my dissertation, everything became a blur because I read the work so many times that I thought I would never want to see this document ever again. Everyone on the committee had different thoughts on where to go with the dissertation and each person had their thoughts on what kinds of changes needed to be done, too. Things seemed so frustrating and difficult, and it was not like anything that I had experienced in my program before. It definitely was not the same as writing a 20-30 page term paper and certainly not like any other course project that I had done before. This was a major undertaking and it seemed like the world was crashing down on me and that there was no light for me to see at the end of the tunnel.

As I went through my dissertation, there were times that I pumped out pages and pages of work and I was really engaged in the material that I was covering. I had spent each night reading about different ways to develop my methodology and creating a comprehensive literature review. This was the usual nighttime activity after I finished work. Each night, I would work diligently to organize my materials and make sure that I covered everything that needed to be included in my literature review and methodology sections. As your study progresses the literature review will help to set the grounding foundation on what information exists on your topic and your job as a researcher, to add to this pile of information. On the flip side of that coin, there were also days that I felt so bogged down and so frustrated that I could not even stand to look at my paper. In some cases, I took a whole week off and, although I don't suggest it, almost took a month off at one point. At different points of my dissertation, I was so overwhelmed by the overall process because I had to jump through so many hoops and keep revising my proposal in order to pass the IRB in order to conduct my study. In some instances, the IRB panel readers were so picky on the words that I used. For example, my use of the word "cold" did not sit well with one of the IRB readers and those minute changes can cause you to take another month in the process because the panel only meets once a month. For me, the major challenges were passing a non-departmentalized Institutional Review Board (IRB), which had been changed at Argosy University and doing all the final touch ups before the final publishing of the dissertation.

For me, breaks during the dissertation process were a blessing in disguise. Although I did not recognize it at that point, those breaks allowed me to recharge my batteries and to take time away from the research so I could look at the study from a different perspective each time I came back to it. When I allowed myself time to get away from the study and allow myself to experience "real life," it really helped me center myself and come back a little more energized and excited each time. During these breaks from research and studying, I would take time to do things that I loved to do, but never had the time to do during my program or just nothing at all to allow my brain time to rest. Although only realizing it now, the dissertation was taking a toll on me and I was forced to re-prioritize my own goals for myself. Maybe, those breaks would include going out for dinner with my friends, going to the gym, watching movies, spending time alone to think, or even going to the beach (I know I am lucky to live in Hawaii.) Although taking a break and dedicating some time for hobbies may seem simple, we are often so caught up in our studies that we do not even have time to enjoy these simple things in life.

These mundane and mindless activities allow our brain to get our minds off stressful situations. Individuals deal with their stress in different ways, and these are some suggestions to help you deal with the stresses that we deal with on an everyday basis during the dissertation process. We all too often get so caught up in making ourselves believe that we don't have enough time because there are too many things to do in a day without taking time to really enjoy some time off for ourselves.

A funny example came in the past year as I was talking to some doctoral students who were in their dissertation process. They were all so tired with their dissertation and were so frustrated with the process of what they were going through. When asked what their goal was, all of them looked at me and agreed that the goal was to get the dissertation done as soon as possible. When I talked to them a little more, it was apparent that they needed to have some time for themselves. Yet, all of the students suggested that it would be counterproductive to take a break despite the fact that all of them would love to have the extra few hours a week to themselves. They were all so focused on their daily activities that they were stuck in the routine of working and did not understand that they were burning themselves out by doing so. What they needed was someone who experienced their struggles to remind them that they would need to change their priorities to help them become more productive. They were so consumed by their routine of continued work that they forgot that their mental and overall health was being compromised. After a little discussion, they promised to take some time off each day to enjoy some of the things that they have missed out in the past few months.

There is always time in a day to do what we want, all we need to do is to prioritize what is most important. All too often, we complain and convince ourselves that we are just too busy with our daily lives. Sometimes, we as human beings need to be reminded to take care of our mind and body first as we want to achieve great things. We, as individuals, tend to be more productive when we have less time on our hands because we know that we do not have time to waste. If we were productive during the times that we were given and left with a little time for enjoyment, those small moments would really mean so much more. It is when we have so much free time that we don't know what to do with ourselves.

As a teacher, this is the mantra that I like to send to my students; we work hard and play hard. If they are productive and self-directed during the day at school, then they should have the rest of the day to enjoy. If they choose to do what they want and waste their time talking to their friends and daydreaming while in school, they will have homework to take home. It is important for them to understand that when they are given time to work, it is always good to practice to setup good work habits so that they learn that through hard work, they can afford the fun activities that they would like to enjoy.

The principals discussed herein extend outside of academia; like a student enduring the dissertation process, there are many things that we would like to do but making time for it can be a challenge. All we need to do is prioritize our goals and make sure that we make time to stay focused and then find time to reward ourselves for our hard work. Finding a balance is an important part of keeping us focused on doing our best in what we do while making sure that we find time to celebrate our accomplishments and for reaching our goals. Our goals may change day by day, week by week, month by month, or even year by year. Know yourself and how much you can push, when to take a step back and when time off is needed. We all need time to just relax and enjoy life. If needed, take time off to make sure that when you work you will be able to produce quality work.

In looking back at myself, I would suggest that dissertational candidates prioritize their goals in ways that best fit their needs. If the goal is to work hard on the dissertation, work hard when you are motivated, but find some time to have "mindless" activities throughout the day to help find balance. These mindless activities could include relaxing, reading for enjoyment, going to the beach, organizing your home, or even just sitting and watching television. Activities that require no higher-level thinking gives your brain a chance to relax. If the goal is to have a little more fun and enjoyment, then take time to have your fun and spend some scheduled time on the dissertation each day. If you need some time off from the process, as I would expect most people do, I would suggest that you should take a day or two off if needed. A dissertation cannot be completed in a day, a week, or even a month and it is a process that will take time.

When I came back to my research after each break I took, I seemed to have a renewed interest in the topic and knew when I was ready to come back and work hard again. This was crucial in getting me through my dissertation as I probably would have crumbled and quit if I did not allow myself to enjoy the simple pleasures of life from time to time.

I do understand that people have their careers and livelihood to worry about, and that tuition can be very pricey so this is why I caution people to only take small breaks from their study. A doctorate degree is very costly and even when you are in the dissertation phase you don't want to waste too much of your time because you are paying tuition for every semester or trimester.

Although I made it out alive, the last two years of my dissertation process was very intensive and, for the most part, I had no life. I was barely able to get enough sleep to go to work and there never seemed to be enough hours in the day to get the things I wanted done. It was a very hard time for me as I enjoy spending time with others and now that I am done, I am making up for all that lost time. I still laugh to this day about the orientation day I had and how that facilitator was so right about a doctorate program being so intensive.

Although I am grateful for that experience and of course that nice piece of paper that says I graduated, I suggest to all doctoral candidates to still take time to prioritize their goals in order to find some sort of balance. There needs to be some time to relax, some time to have fun, and some time to work. The demands of life come at us in different ways and at different times, and the goal is to make sure that we prioritize our goals in a way that makes best sense given our current situation.

The Hard Truth

Going through the dissertation process can be a long and arduous process. It usually takes people a couple of years to complete and signifies that they are an expert in their field through their contributions to the existing literature. The process can frustrate many people and, as you may already know, this is the stage where many students decide to quit and have the term ABD (all but dissertation) next to their name. The dissertation which is the final piece of literature, serves as a right of passage in completing a person's doctoral study and signifies that they are now in a special class of researchers, which makes them a doctor of their specialty.

The process is tough and the road will at times be rocky. This is why sometimes, you need to enjoy the ride and enjoy life. It is impossible for anyone to keep working day after day, 365 days a year and be satisfied with their accomplishments. For this reason, many people choose to enjoy their time off of work and go on vacations with friends and family. What would life be if we only worked all the time? No fun of course.

Although we would like our dissertation to only take us a few months, the reality of it is that it may even take us a lot longer than that only to get our proposal through our IRB. Although a sad reality, there are appropriate times to take your breaks properly and prioritize your goals in life. We must strive to separate ourselves from the study and give ourselves time to be rejuvenated to maximize further learning and work. When you come back from a short rest, it allows you to be a little more open minded about the different suggestions that may come from your committee. A break also allows you to see the data or your literature review from a different perspective when you are not reading the same material over and over.

Like having a job in the real world, people always find time to spend with their families and friends in order to unwind from a stressful work and life situation. Through prioritizing our goals, we make time to do the things that we want to do and sometimes need to sacrifice other things to do so. The dissertation process is no different and we need to allow ourselves some time out especially if you are balancing your dissertation with a full-time job. It can be very stressful balancing the demands of a full-time job and adding on the demands of a doctoral program. Both of these can really put a toll on you both physically and mentally and you need to find ways to have some down time to relax your mind and ease your stress levels.

For some people, they find it comforting to relax and be with family and have open conversations about anything other than school, just take time off to relax for a few days, or to speak with colleagues who may spark more interesting academic conversations about other types of research. In some cases, some people who are going through these stresses find support groups to help them cope with the stress. One good way to help alleviate some of the stresses is to meet up with fellow students who are going through the same stresses as you are and form a support group. By having a support group, you not only meet new people but understand that you are not the only one who is going through the long and frustrating process, and there are others who can help you along the way. This is especially important when things get rough and you have someone there who can relate to the same stresses that you are going through.

At Argosy University, there is now a support group that meets once a month to help support students who may be having trouble navigating themselves through the doctoral program itself or the dissertation process. At each meeting, the members try to invite different speakers to talk about their experiences in the program and offer words of advice to help students who are struggling in the program. I am honored to have been invited to one of these meetings and it was great to share some of the ideas in this book with those in attendance. Some of my chapters have even come from different questions that were raised by students at these support meetings.

It is important to have a social support system in place and to have someone there to rely on to keep you motivated throughout the process. Time spent with a support group away from the dissertation to relax and open your mind to different things can be just as helpful as going out and having fun. These people are there to keep you focused on the main goal of graduating and to help you release tension in your time of need. Everyone will need someone there to keep them on track, especially while hitting the different bumps in the road along the way.

Life has a way of teaching us that we cannot have everything that we want. If we do want certain things, there may be an opportunity cost for it and certain things need to be sacrificed. We must learn to make the best of what we have and to learn that through prioritizing our needs, we will be able to get what we want. We must seek a balance between work and play and find time to enjoy the life that we have.

Lessons Learned

1. When you feel defeated, take time out for yourself and come back with a renewed sense of vision.
2. Prioritize your current goals and make time for the things you need to.
3. You are never alone. Your feelings of frustration are normal.
4. Find a support group at school to help with some of your uncertainties.

Jamie Dela Cruz

Chapter 8- Don't Rush or Make Assumptions

As you go through your research I want to emphasize the importance of carrying a journal or a notebook daily. Having a notebook will help you to write down any awkwardness in conversation or any special notations of which you believe are important during your interviews. These notations will help you to remember which of the participants you may want to have private conversations with to help clarify any areas of uncertainty. Private conversations will also ensure that you record all the details that participants may have wanted to share with you but hadn't, especially if you are conducting group interviews where some people may be a little apprehensive to share their ideas in front of others. In addition, notes help to understand the true feelings of each participant in order to correctly interpret responses that are made by each subject while not bringing any personal biases into the analysis.

As you continue to interview your participants, following up with these notations is important so that participants are given the proper opportunity to voice their opinions in a safe environment. In this effort, they are likely to feel that their narrative will be valued and taken for what it is worth while not feeling as though they are under evaluation. In doing so, this will alleviate many problems that require you to piece together their responses and decide where they stand on a particular subject especially if their responses tend to be very vague. In phenomenology, even those who may not be "story worthy" are still good candidates for participation. However, some participants may need a little more guided discovery than others.

We must remember that phenomenology is a learning experience to better understand the lived experiences through people, the participants and their stories. Like students in school, participants are learning how to best articulate their stories by recollecting all of their experiences into short sessions of interviewing. They will also need guidance from you, the researcher, to help them best explain their thoughts. Please remember that they can be successful as you help them to understand their roles as participants, and as you help them uncover their meaningful experiences. As researchers in phenomenological studies, it is important for you to obtain as much detail from your participants as possible to ensure there is no confusion understanding their intended message. This way, you are not forced to come to your own conclusions on what they meant in the transcriptions of the interviews.

To ensure that my data was both valid and reliable within my dissertation study, I took notes, using the approaches that were mentioned in this chapter along with recording the responses of each participant. In addition, I asked my participants to review their transcriptions after each interview by adding or retracting any statements that were made during the interviewing process. Since I was the primary source of data collection, it was important for me to acknowledge potential personal biases at the beginning of the study in order to freely analyze the degree to which those biases may have impacted the data analysis. If any discrepancies were flagged in the transcriptions that each participant was asked to review, I clarified statements with the participants to see whether these were their intended message (this was a very important step that helped alleviate much of the headache of misinterpreted information as many participants actually added to their original answers.) Vital for me was being cognizant of the factors that may have affected the presentation of the responses of the participants while ensuring that emerging themes were correctly identified through the interview and process of analysis.

When conducting my research of a Hawaiian culture-based curriculum, I felt that I wanted to point out all of the great things about the curriculum after the initial focus-group interview with all of my participating teachers. After reviewing all of my responses to my initial questions in my focus-group interview, what I noticed was that teachers seemed to love the curriculum given a few tweaks of their own. Following the review process for the focus group, I believed that my participants' lived experiences were positive ones. I thought to myself, *why would I not decide otherwise?* I looked over my data many times and saw the same themes arise from it.

I began writing new probing questions for my participants' second individual interviews. For the secondary interviews, I planned on further exploring their experiences and allowing them to share any experiences that they were not able to share or were not able to recall during the first interview session. I was very excited about all of these great experiences and thought that the interview process would be so great to explore all of the positive experiences that these teachers had with the curriculum. I told myself that I would to be prepared for the second interview and would be ready with my questions a month before interviewing the teachers again at the end of the semester.

When I brought forth my questions to my committee members, they were very weary about my intended direction and approach. All of my participants were expecting to have more in-depth questions that not only looked at the positive experiences of these teachers but also inquired if there were any negative experiences with the culture-based curriculum. After a quick analysis of the situation, I realized that I did not stop to think about the possibility that these teachers might have also undergone a negative experience with the curriculum even though these feelings did not surface during the initial interview.

After coming up with some new questions, I was intrigued by the kinds of new possible avenues that I could further explore with my participants. Night after night, I thought of new questions to ask my participating teachers. After about a week, I brought my new set of questions to my committee members and worked with them to refine these questions. For me, it was an enlightening experience to see the different perspectives of each evaluator on where to take this study. Although it can be a very frustrating experience working with each committee member and integrating their thoughts to make a final decision, it can be a very positive experience if you are willing to keep an open mind to their opinions. Members of your dissertation committee are there to help you. However, I believe that as you move further along with your dissertation, you must be able to make the critical decision of where you want to go with your study and to decide what questions will be most important to get a fair analysis of the situation.

Like any other qualitative study and evaluations of programs, it is important to make sure that you do create a holistic picture of the situation. As in the case of my dissertation, I was forced to explore both sides of the coin and discovered that many other experiences were not brought to my attention the first time through the initial interview. Pointing this out is not intended to blame my participants. However, this is where you as a researcher need to help your participants best explain their experiences so that you can get a better picture of what really happened. Without the proper guidance of my dissertation committee, I would have gone through the whole dissertation thinking that this was the most amazing curriculum that made such a positive impact on this school. I am not merely expressing that it wasn't a positive experience, but I would not have had a balanced approach to the situation, which may have reduced the validity and reliability of my study.

In understanding my shortfall at an important stage in my own dissertation, I would like to caution emerging researchers to not make the same mistake. Many of us in the dissertation at a certain point want to complete our study as soon as possible, collect the data and be done with the paper. As much as I wanted to complete my paper, I was always cautioned by one of my committee members that we must strive to do the work right at the doctoral level as this publication can go a long way toward finding you a job in the future.

As I moved further along with the process of data collection and did my second round of interviews, I found myself having longer-than-expected conversations with my study's participants. My second round of interviews served to better understand the teacher's experiences with the curriculum and to probe them for a better understanding of their experiences in a more confidential environment. In doing my interviews, I was so fascinated to see so many different responses to their struggles with the curriculum as I initially thought that I was going to explore all of the positive experiences. Through having one-on-one sessions, this intimate setting allowed some of the teachers to freely express their concerns about the program, knowing that what they said would not be criticized by the others in the group. This style of interviewing can be more comfortable for many participants who may need more time to formulate answers in their mind or who may be shy from expressing their true feelings in front of others in fear of ridicule from the group.

Interview after interview, I was able to better understand the complexities that existed in their experiences. Although my participants enjoyed their experience with the curriculum, there were so many underlying issues that were not brought forward in the first focus-group interview. For example, many of these teachers were not from Hawaii. Although these teachers enjoyed having these experiences with the curriculum while students were certainly having positive learning experiences with the curriculum, they were not completely comfortable using the curriculum. Some of these teachers who were not from Hawaii had a difficult time with the pronunciation of the Hawaiian vocabulary words within the curriculum. Others had a hard time explaining the history of the place as they were foreign to it, which is critical to the culture-based aspect of the curriculum.

What then became the challenge was to articulate these setbacks while making sure that I completely understood them before I was able to make conclusions on their responses. Here in lies another important lessons learned. It is best to completely understand the issues at hand before making generalizations about statements that are made by participants in your study. In doing so, you will not misrepresent your subjects and will not make false statements that you wanted to see instead of making sure that they are supported by multiple participants.

For my study, I was able to maintain a high level of reliability by making sure that each of my participants were able to review their transcriptions after each interview. In doing so, participant teachers were able to read their statements, add any other relevant information that they felt was necessary, retract any statements that they did not want to say publicly, or add any other relevant data to the entire transcription that they felt was necessary after the interview was completed.

When all of the transcriptions were completed, I put the statements into a graphic organizer to organize the different responses into different themes that emerged during my review of the responses. Some of the responses were omitted. Some of the responses were retained depending on the number of responses that were in a category. This organization of data can be the most frustrating part of the whole experience because there is no one way to organize data in qualitative studies, especially that of phenomenology. Depending on your sample size, you may possibly be looking at 15-20 different responses for one question with each of the responses likely going in different tangents. Picking out those responses that stand out to you as most important is a challenge and can take you for a long ride.

If you know that organization is not your best skill, find a way to organize the data that makes most sense for you. There are many different graphic organizers that are recommended by other professionals to help you sort out your data. However, you should find one that allows you to see the emerging themes that stand on their own or may possibly be overlapping with other themes. It is then that you will learn to break the themes apart to create ones that really stand out as important for your research.

Day after day, I looked at the data and saw new themes arise and old ones fall apart. The trick for me was to look at all of the data for a day and spend hours and hours reviewing it, organizing the data into themes that I felt was right. For me, it was important to take a few days off so I could take my mind off of it. After doing so, I was able to resume reviewing my data again to see if I had the same feelings about it. On some days the more I looked at the data, the more frustrated I became requiring me to I put my things away for a moment. I waited for another day when I was able to think a little clearer. On some days I wanted to make things happen and jump to writing the analysis but stayed the course and tried my best to keep sight of what was important.

Patience here is a critical component of making a good analysis while making sure that you are able to present the most valid information in the most organized and complete manner.

As I look back on the experience, I feel that this piece of information was crucial to my success in the dissertation phase of my program of study. In understanding that patience is so important in making great connections, I believe that by taking the time to do things well and learning a craft well from others who are willingly spending time to train us, will not only carry into our daily lives but will help us when we try to find jobs of our own. As a recent graduate, I feel that this experience should not be taken lightly. Although this is a culminating experience, we are still students who continue to learn throughout our lives. The lessons I learned through my dissertation have allowed me to become more effective in evaluating programs through the phenomenological methodology. These lessons have really set me up to become more independent in my endeavors. I feel much more confident now than I did coming into the dissertation project.

I have undergone transformations due to experiences from my study and have seen the wonderful impact that this curriculum has resulted on student achievement. Additionally, my participants who were interviewed showed me how much they care about their students. They also demonstrated the amount of commitment teachers need to have in order to learn and implement a culture-based curriculum well. My research has not only showed me the reasons why these teachers have loved this curriculum but has given me the example that I in my role as an educator want to follow as I continue my career as a classroom teacher.

The Truth

Many of us have heard old adages regarding patience:

"Have patience, my friend, have patience;

For Rome wasn't built in a day!

You wear yourself out for nothing

In many and many a way! Why are you nervous and fretty

When things do not move along fast;

Why let yourself get excited

Over things that will soon be past?"

Critical Writing: Stories as Phenomena

- Gertrude Tooley Buckingham

Whether the adage was said by our parents or grandparents, we have heard this statement—over and over again. As irritating as this adage may have sounded—words that we have taken for granted—we learn to live by these wise words, which have become more important as we have grown up. Many of us have even used these words with our own children as we became grown-ups. How ironic!

When conducting phenomenological studies, the old adage still remains true. Through my experience of doing my dissertation, I have learned that being patient does pay off. As researchers of qualitative studies, we must be patient and allow themes to emerge from the data. However, it is important not to rush any processes and not to rush the creation of themes that we may want to materialize in our analysis. Rushing can prove to be the most damaging mistake to make while creating phenomenological studies, which was the mistake that I almost fell victim to, myself.

It may take you a week or perhaps a month to process all the collected data before you are able to write an analysis and come to any conclusions. However, the important thing is to take your time to make sure that you are thoroughly presenting your information. As the researcher in the dissertation, you alone will have your transcriptions. Your job will be ensuring that you are able to categorize your data in a way that makes the most sense to you. As I look back, I should have written more detailed journal entries to keep track of my feelings and ideas that floated through my mind during the study. Detailed journal entries could've later served as reminders of what kinds of things I thought about before returning to review the data. Having journal entries to reference would have made the process a little easier while tracking the different themes that I saw arise and fall apart, along with providing me reasons as to why such occurred.

The skill of putting the informational pieces together is the glue of that makes phenomenological puzzles "stick." The interviews can be such amazing experience as we learn from the experiences of others while probing for more information—this can be tricky. But the way to organize and present our material is the key to moving forward. Through planned out, well-implemented and sound reliability and validity testing and strong analysis skills, good things can come out from phenomenological studies. Phenomenology as a type of qualitative inquiry not only impacts those around us who are able to access the studies online, but also affects the researcher. As we walk away from these research studies, whether we know it or not, we are changed by the process as we have learned something new from the experiences of others. This herein lies the true power of phenomenological study whereby the researcher and subjects are forever changed by talking about and exploring the experiences of subjects under a specific situation. This is the benefit of doing phenomenological studies where both parties are able to learn from the same experience. Thus, the participant is able to experience self-realization in better understanding the experience and better learning from things that they may not have realized in order to make their practices more efficient or effective. In contrast, the researcher is able to not only understand and learn from their experiences, but is able to properly share and articulate their story so that others can learn from the experience as well.

As we work with different groups of people who would like to use our expertise, it is important that we learn to approach them in ways that are respectful. With this understanding, there needs to be common ground where the participants in the study are open and willing to share their ideas in order to make these kinds of studies successful. For me, I really believe that by stating mutual agreements from the beginning and having a common understanding of the goals of the study, it helps organizations move forward. In my experience, I like organizations to know that the role of a researcher is not to evaluate each person but to learn from their experiences and chat with them about their experiences to help them become more efficient.

We work in a busy world where everyone has a million things to do each day. In understanding this, it is important that we learn to respect people's time during our research. We do know that we will never be able to fully compensate our participants for their time through money since they will be volunteering to be a part of the study. Finding ways to make the experience beneficial for the participants in other ways is important. These could include allowing participants to better understand themselves, help them to professionally develop, or even allow the project to be a part of a project at work or to help their organization create an improvement plan. In this way, the participants and administration can feel that their participation in the study will help them upon completing the interviews. In my study, the participating teachers used my report to help with their accreditation plan toward showing that the culture-based curricula works within an educational setting. My final report also documented the continued professional development that their teachers did in their classroom to help build effective curricula for their students.

In making these conscious efforts, your participants will have a vested interest in your project and will feel that they want to share more with you in knowing that there is a return for themselves as well. In doing so, participants' organizations can receive better feedback on how to improve programs or ways that their organizations can best support their field. This is an important component of a phenomenological study as participants are able to share their true feelings with the researcher in the hopes of creating an awareness. This awareness not only enables learning for participants but also enables learning of others from the same experience as well. From this experience, participants learn that they go beyond just sharing just to share their experience. In fact, they learn that they are empowered to help themselves better understand their experience so that they can either better cope with the overall situation, become more effective in what they do, or even to make themselves better people as a whole. Of course, all of such, depends on your study and what you are trying to research.

It is with hope that through expressing their feelings, your subjects are able to reach a level of self-realization of areas to foster greater learning. As they partake in this journey, participants not only learn from their experiences but help others to learn from it as well so that others do not also make the same mistakes. On the flip side, such experiences serve as references. Through these experiences, people can appreciate the good that can be learned so that they can try to replicate them for themselves.

As a researcher, I too have very much to learn from these experiences. What I realized was that through these experiences, we learn how to work with people under distress, how to probe for more information from participants, read body language, understand needs, and how to keep meaningful conversations ongoing. As we continue to do more interviews, we learn that the learning does not only occur with the participant but is also carried along in their journey. We learn to make sense of the participants' responses and internalize their negative and positive feelings about their experiences. Doing so helps participants to better understand the overall experience and to create a learning environment from it.

Lessons Learned

1. Take time to explore the positives and negatives.
2. Stay the course. Be patient when you analyze your data.
3. Take time to do your own learning from the experiences and have personal take-aways as you reflect upon the responses from your participants as well as your notes throughout the interview.

4. Be a good guide for your participants.

Chapter 9 - Owning Your Dissertation

Throughout the dissertation process, I always thought that the only way to get through the process was to follow the literal directions given by the committee. This was the approach that I took as I went through my own dissertation journey. Following committee directions is also the way that many other colleagues I know got through the process. It seemed very simple; when your committee told you to add more content to your dissertation you did as they requested and went along your merry way. In most cases, I understood the committee's motives and reasoning for adding in particular portions to the dissertation. I also understood why they want to make sure that my literature review and methodology sections were well-structured. For many of the suggestions in the literature review and methodology sections, it was critical that I not only laid out all of the information that was set before my study but also set up the literature review in such a way that would help me better understand my topic so I could get a more holistic view. It is with hope that you have done some case studies within your own program and you can see how important it is to have a broader understanding of your topic at hand.

As I moved further along with the dissertation and moved on to my analysis and conclusions, my committee continued to give me what I considered great guidance. I listened to their rationale behind making a complete evaluation of the curriculum based on what they saw in my writing and decided that, because they were experts in the field, that they knew what was best. They helped me to make sense of the themes that I saw and helped me to clarify those areas with different suggestions. I continued on this path and scheduled the final defense of my proposal.

The challenge at this point in the dissertation was for me to really hone down on the skills that I learned in my qualitative classes during my doctorate program. For me, I found that the class work I completed in my qualitative research methods class, as well as ones in program evaluation, were critical in helping me to continue to refine the skills that I have learned and developed in my program. In our program evaluation classes, we used qualitative methods to work with local organizations like the YMCA. We applied qualitative methods to help them understand their needs in to hiring and retaining great employees and to help them find suggestions that would refine their hiring and retention practices. By participating in projects based on real-world case studies during the program, I felt confident I would be able to tackle the kinds of problems that I did in my dissertation, especially when I got to difficult problems in the process.

The dissertation process is very challenging. In reflecting on my experiences now, I feel that it was well worth the extra effort to gain proper and situationally applicable experiences, and to collaborate with my committee members in the same way that I was able to with my team mates in my program evaluation classes to come up with new ideas and conclusions for the YMCA. Seeing things from their point of view—an external point of view outside of my own—really helped me to make better sense of the material in front of me.

Taking my committee's advice seemed like a logical plan and through learning and understanding how I could best put forth my dissertation, I would be done in the fastest possible way. As many of you continue on your dissertation journey, you will come to know exactly what I am talking about, if you haven't already. You have seen and read your paper so many times over that everything seems to read perfectly because it makes perfect sense in your head. Regardless of thinking my work read perfectly, any suggestions for further improvement were taken to heart and changes were made based upon what my committee thought needed improvement.

What I found to be frustrating is that other readers, especially my committee members, were not always able to make the same connections to my understandings on the subject. Understand that they may have this difficulty in making sense of your analysis because they do not have the same perspective as you do because they were not exposed to the same experiences and data that you were. Your committee members are putting the puzzle pieces together and trying to make sense of what you may have seen in the data based on your write up. Through this understanding, they try to help you to create a better understanding of the situation in order for you to best articulate your analysis. Committee members can play an important role in the way that your dissertation is done. They will have lots of great advice to help guide you in creating a great study. In stating this, there will be times where you will reach out to your committee members for help in formulating your themes, but please remember that you are the only one who has sat in the interviews and collected the data. Getting knowledge firsthand and traveling with your participants throughout their journey is something that cannot be replaced.

As you take the stories in during your interviews and relay them to your committee, be assertive about what you have seen and stand up for yourself when you truly believe that their suggestions may not lead you in the direction that you feel is right. This is why I encourage all of you to take detailed notes about what you hear and experience while gathering field data from interviews. Be sure that your notes go beyond just what they are telling you. Subtle clues like fidgeting, their uneasiness, and their passion about their stories can all be explored through a great researcher, like you. In some cases, committee members may try to guide you to make suggestions on final themes that they hear you gravitating toward, but make sure that you are comfortable with their suggestions before moving forward.

Once everything was set and I was getting ready to defend my final dissertation, one of my committee members challenged my thinking and asked if I was completely satisfied with my results. The committee member continued to explain that she felt that I was just following the guidance that was given to me by the committee and she didn't know if I completely understood why certain changes were being made. I continued to reply that at our school, this process of taking advice seemed to be the norm at our university and that was the wisdom that many of the students who had graduated prior to me have passed on to students who were entering their dissertation phase. This reply was to alleviate any further conflict that would arise within the committee whereby students are learners and teachers are experts in the field they are studying.

For me, it was a very enlightening experience for someone to ask me my opinion of the situation. Throughout my study, I was used to asking everyone else for their experience and expertise and this turn in questioning really struck me as being an important part of my dissertation. Although this question came a little late in my dissertational process, I was glad that it happened because it sparked a new realization for me that what I did think about the project was really important and that there was some value in my thoughts.

In looking back at the dissertation experience, this is what has inspired me to really think about my experiences as a doctoral student. These are the kind of experiences that a student who is in their dissertation phase should have. Although this committee member did challenge me in other ways to take ownership of my dissertation, it was only through having this one conversation that I realized how important and valuable my experience could have been if we had chosen to be more collaborative in our efforts. Students should feel like they have more of an active role in their dissertations and should not shy away from these types of experiences that could really help them to better analyze their understandings of their study. In addition, students also take control of the areas that interest them and help to guide where their study will go.

Though it may feel that the only way to get through the dissertation is to follow the guidance of our committee members, please take caution about saying everything the committee tells you to. Think about all of the things that you have learned in your program. Reflect on whether or not every idea being presented—yours and the committee's—makes sense to you. If something does not make sense, don't be ashamed to ask questions to make sure that you are not completely lost in the whole process. This is your story to share and you need to share a story that you are comfortable with.

In my case, my methodology was something that was completely new to me, and I was trying to make sense of it when writing up the methodology section. I feel that while learning about the phenomenological model, I could have been more confident in myself and my understanding of it. Perhaps confidence was what I needed to be able to have a dialogue with my committee members instead of trying to always go through the motions and following their lead in this process. Confidence could have made my life a little easier as I prepared for my proposal defense and answered their questions then. In my case, I was a little afraid to ask questions because some of the personalities of my committee members were quite strong and they seemed to expect you to already know a lot about your methodology before your study started. In my program, we did not start our dissertation research in previous classes, therefore starting my dissertation and going through all of the materials was new. I know that my friends who attended other universities started their research in earlier course work that helped to create a smoother transition into their dissertation.

For me, I had one committee member who was very influential on our campus and who also had a very strong personality. In having this person on the committee, I didn't feel comfortable sharing opinions and because of this, I felt a need to rely more heavily on their advice and not on my own instincts. Although this was not at a complete loss and I did learn a lot from their insights as researchers and program evaluators, I feel that a lot more could have been accomplished and learned through a more collaborative effort. In understanding the role of a dissertation-researching student, you are in a sense an equal counterpart to your committee members. As a counterpart to your committee, feel free to share your thoughts as if you were an expert in the field and knowledgeable about the data that was collected. Through their help, your understanding of your participants' experiences can become clearer and can help you to further develop your study and guide you in ways that may spark your interest. In this way you can take your study to different "arenas" and be able to possibly explore your topic in different tangents that may lead you to have new discoveries that you never thought possible when you first started out.

Like the qualitative research models, we are the sole researcher in the study. We do not have anyone to refer back to in case we are lost and thus our job as researchers is very important. In understanding this, it is important that we are fully engaged in our projects to be able to paint an accurate representation of the experiences of our participants. Through a collaborative effort, the researcher's role should not be underestimated and should have an equal presence within the team collaboration.

Looking back at this experience, I feel that I could have been more of an active participant in the dissertation process and could have stood up more for where I felt the dissertation could have gone. In many cases, I did think that some of the changes were unnecessary and although I did feel strongly about not changing certain aspects of the dissertation, I went along with the changes that my committee felt were necessary. As minute as they could have been, I feel that it is important that students in this process should feel that their voice is valued and one that should be respected. Of course, there are places where committee suggestions should be justifiably added, but there should be open communication channels where you feel that you can express your opinions.

Everyone deals with ideas of perception differently. What happened to me was that each of my committee members had their own perception of where the study should go depending on their background and experiences. Each went into their own tangents that they felt were most important, not keeping in mind that it was not really their journey to take. Although I am thankful for their help and guidance, I think that my experience could have been different had I been afforded the opportunity to do more exploration with their guidance.

I can only imagine what my study could have looked like had we came together as a unified group of individuals toward a single goal instead of having differing perspectives of where the dissertation could go. Through these efforts, it could have offered an opportunity for me to have a more meaningful experience through the dissertation process and allowed me to have a deeper appreciation for each participant's voice. Like my reflection of my dissertation now, these experiences can provide researchers the means to connect with their participants on a deeper level if they are pushed to better understand themselves and the ways that interviewing can unlock a meaningful experience in their lives. Through writing this "story" and hearing the voices of my committee members, I am now more aware of how fragile these experiences can be as I learn to question myself and the ways in which my dissertational experiences have affected me.

As you move on to your findings and analysis, I think that there is no better advice than to trust your instincts and stand up for what you see in the data. Do not make the same mistake that I did and allow your committee members to shape your dissertation especially if what they suggest does not correspond to your research purposes. I was lucky however that my committee was able to read into my initial analysis and helped me to organize my themes into broader and more descriptive categories.

If you choose to follow in my footsteps and find yourself allowing your committee to help shape your project, I would suggest that you be able to clearly articulate participant responses so that they can help to guide you in the right direction. In doing so, they are basing their assistance on the data that you are presenting them with and will help you to create an evaluation of the experiences that you have learned. In working with them, they will be able to help you to formulate more meaningful conclusions based on your experiences with your participants that you may not have initially thought about.

I am not saying that this strategy—giving the committee members a dominant role in your dissertation—will not work but may not provide you with the richest learning environment by which you may best learn from. I really believe that it depends on your learning style and ways that you are best able to learn from others and what they have to offer. Some people like others to tell them what needs to be done and this approach may fit their learning style best. Others may want people to involve them in the process and allow room for critical thinking about the dissertation. Find your comfort level and find those qualities that best suit you while working with your committee members for your dissertation.

Each of us tend to teach others in ways that best suit our own learning style and I was lucky enough to have different teaching styles present themselves from members on my committee; styles to offer me different perspectives. In my case, one member was a little more dominant than the other committee members and compelled me to go in one direction. It is with hope that your committee will be a little more accommodating to your style of learning and provide you with the best learning environment.

So in looking for a committee, be sure to find people who you feel you connect well with. These people need to have some flexibility in working with not only you, but the other committee members that will be a part of the committee team. These individuals are critical in the success of your dissertation and it is important to know each person's strengths in order for them to best help you.

My suggestion to all of you as budding researchers is to make a promise to yourself that you will become active participants in your own study. When things do not make sense to you make sure that your questions are answered. In addition, if there are any changes that you do not feel are necessary, that you stand up for yourself and make sure that before a change is made, that it is done in the best interest of your study. Finally, take all suggestions with a grain of salt. In many cases, your committee members are merely suggesting changes to you and as a researcher you should be ready to make those tough decisions as you move along. This will help you as you move along in your career when you do have to make those decisions on your own.

The Truth

The dissertation is a time for you to get comfortable with your talents as a researcher and it important that you learn your craft well. During this time, you are learning how to do real-world research on your own and finding ways to make your process more efficient. This is the time when you are able to use the methodology that you learned during your coursework and where you can apply it to a case study of your choice.

As you formulate meaning from your research, it is important that you spend the needed time with your data in order to make the critical decisions that you will face as you move forward in your career. As the sole investigator of your phenomenological study, you are the only researcher who really understands the intricacies of the data. You have sat with your participants, heard every word that they had to say, and have seen their expressions as they were making their responses to the questions that you prepared for them. You have spent hours and hours with your data and taken notes about what you have heard. And no one else will have as in-depth knowledge of the data as you do.

When you feel that you have done a great analysis, you may need to seek the advice of your committee members who may be able to guide you in certain directions that may help you to better elaborate on your thoughts. This can be very insightful information as the terminologies can be very important, especially if you are in the evaluation field like me. These collaboration times can be very productive and these more experienced people in your field can help you make your thoughts more concise. Furthermore, collaboration with field experts will help you really hone down your presentation of your study.

Although it may be comforting knowing that you have your committee members to depend on if you are having a hard time, it is important that you feel comfortable with your final writing and allow your committee members to only assist you in your times of need. It is not expected that during this dissertation that you are going to be able to produce the entire paper on your own and your committee members do understand that you will need some assistance from time to time. Remember that you are still a student and that you will still have many things to learn even after you are completed with your dissertation. This dissertation helps students to become more independent in their work and helps you to highlight your skills as a researcher before you are sent into the "real world" of work.

Remember that as a doctoral candidate ready to finish their dissertation, you have a lot to offer. Although we may not be a full-fledged doctor yet, our opinions do matter. We should be afforded the opportunity to share our ideas in a professional way and to learn from the opinions of others. In having a collaborative approach, we are afforded new opportunities for learning where meaningful conversations can be had that can build further learning.

In conclusion, be confident in your skills as a researcher and make sure to be comfortable with any changes made to your dissertation. If your committee feels that changes need to be made, be sure to stick to your guns especially when you feel confident with your analysis and conclusions. You are the expert on the data and hear out their suggestions and plead your case if you do not agree with any changes.

Lessons Learned

1. Let YOUR voice be heard.
2. The dissertation process should be a collaborative effort with field experts.
3. We can also learn about ourselves in this process.
4. Stand up for what you believe!

Chapter 10 - Defending the Dissertation

Defending your dissertation is one of the most important parts of your dissertation and will signify whether or not your study has passed the approval of your committee to move forward. This is not the final step as you will still be asked to revise a few areas within your dissertation when this process is over and you will also be asked to get your paper edited professionally before the final binding stage. Please understand that this is another—and one of the final—benchmarks on finishing up your dissertation.

As I reflect on my own experience I would like to encourage you to really take this component very seriously. I have seen and have had the luxury of sitting in a few defenses before I defended my own to help prepare me for the kinds of challenges that may lay ahead. In sitting in these defenses, there were some that went very smoothly, that ended very positively and you could tell that they really understood all five chapters of their study well. They were able to show that they understood their study from the guiding questions, literature review, methodology and results to the summary, discussion and further research. In other defenses, I could definitely tell that some of the researchers were unfamiliar with their own study. They couldn't provide enough to convey to their committee that they really understood their own literature review as well as their results, which are critical components of a well-thought-out dissertation.

If you are thinking to yourself that everyone passes as you would expect and that your committee has already asked you difficult questions during the process, you are definitely mistaken. During your defense you will be asked many questions based on your dissertation that your committee has already read. In many cases, they will ask you to reiterate some of the same questions that they feel you may not know very well to ensure that you know your study well. In my own defense, I felt that I was asked many other clarifying questions especially in the area of where I could possibly take my study if I were to expand it in the future.

My committee members always reminded me that when doing a study within a university setting that you can't always conduct a study the way that you might want to do it within a private organization because of the IRB and the ways that they will regulate studies. As I did my own study within the Argosy system I found this to be very true and I felt that we were tiptoeing around asking questions that I felt could have really captured a different perspective and allowed me to explore different tangents of my study but because the study is very focused it helped me to keep focused on doing a few aspects well.

As I look back upon the discussions that I had with my committee members, they really did keep things in perspective for me. In the beginning I really felt that I wanted to tackle many different challenges that came up within my literature review and my committee members always reminded me to always stick to my overarching questions because in qualitative research, things may not always go in the direction that you may foresee. As you start to interview your participants you may be drawn in more than one direction and you may start to explore different areas that you did not foresee coming up. If you choose too many tangents and those tangents take you in many more directions, you may find yourself in a bad place trying to take on too much.

I would suggest that when going into the room to present your defense to your committee members, try to make sure that you have notes within the PowerPoint or presentation slides or on note cards to make sure that you really emphasize points that you feel are most important. As I sat in many of these defenses I observed that each person has their own way that they feel most comfortable. Some researchers like to print out their slides and notes and some people tend to use index cards. In many cases, since you have already defended your proposal in the first chapters of your dissertation it should be very easy for you to talk about your study, but sometimes we forget the simple parts that we take for granted. This is one point that is especially important for many researchers to consider. Even in my own case I would explain my study to people as if they had already read my paper and knew about my study. I feel that this happened because as you discuss these topics with your chair or with committee members you take for granted that they have been a part of this process for over a year and they have heard about the many aspects of your project already. To those outside of this bubble, it could be very confusing if you do not lay the foundation for anyone to understand what your study would be about.

Luckily for me, I had a lot of great friends—some who were also in the program and some who were educators—willing to observe me conduct practice presentations were I would also try to explain my topic to them. In this way, these people who did not know anything about my study could critique my mock defense to see the questions that the committee might ask me, too. The questions my friends voiced became pointers of where I needed to better explain when I did the real presentation before the committee. The practice presentations were very important for me and I felt that it helped me the most in making sure that I was able to communicate most effectively. These practice presentations will also prepare you in the case there are other people from your university there in the room who may sit in.

From what I have seen, each university has different policies on who may sit in your presentation. For me, I had my committee members as well as the chair of my department. In other universities, the dean of the university and other faculty members may come in to see how things are going. I know that this can be an overwhelming day but don't feel overwhelmed if more people come in. From my experience they are generally there to help you and will not be a part of the evaluation process, anyway.

As you wrap up your presentation, your committee members will have one final chance to provide you with any further questions that they feel necessary. There are so many kinds of questions that could arise, but knowing your study is so critical in being successful in this stage of your dissertation. In my case, my committee members asked questions to find ways for me to build upon possible ways I could expand on my study if I had the time and less restrictions of doing a research study within a university setting.

These were such great ideas for me to think about which I had not thought about before finishing my study and threw me for a curveball. In my study, I thought that by doing my final chapter on discussions and further research I had covered my bases and knew where I could take my study, but the committee challenged me to really take that understanding to a new level. Sometimes we can get so caught up in our study that we don't always think about different avenues for success and get stuck in confinements of university studying. We don't always think about the bigger picture of other studies that are possible.

This is also how they got me thinking about how I could do more writing in the future and to possibly present my findings at a conference. All of these discussions have really helped me to be more confident in ways that I was able to continue my research and take on new challenges as an evaluator and consultant to different organizations. When I completed my work, I was still unsure of what kind of positions I could realistically take on with this kind of dissertation and it really gave me the confidence to get myself out there and share my talents with companies in my local community.

When you are done answering the committee's questions—possibly a very heart wrenching process—your committee will then allow you to leave the room and they will have their deliberation time. When they deliberate, they will discuss how well you did in your presentation. They will discuss how well-prepared you were and if the presentation satisfied the criteria for getting through the defense. Usually this will take about 30 minutes to an hour and it can be very scary, especially if they ask you very tough questions at the end of your presentation and you don't know how well you covered all of your points.

Generally, most universities will offer students 3 different outcomes. One would be that you fully pass the defense, two being you could pass with conditions that you change some parts of the paper to clarify points, or three a no pass. In most of the cases that I have heard about, including my own, most people pass with conditions that certain parts be changed. The purpose of implementing the changes is to allow you to fully reflect upon the experience and to solidify points that may have not been complete.

If you did very well and get a pass, you move on to the next phase of the dissertation. If you do get a conditional pass you have to fix those components discussed in the debrief when they call you back into the room and then move to the next phase after their approval. If you did not pass you have to do the entire defense of your dissertation again.

As you move on to the next phase many researchers believe that they have completed their program and they are ready for graduation. This is not true and there is still more that goes with your dissertation. From here you would still need to get your study reviewed and edited by a professional editor. Generally, editors for dissertations charge about three to five dollars a page for review and they will do the final read-through and editing for errors especially in the writing format that your college accepts (i.e. MLA, APA, etc.). This is great for catching minute errors that you may not have picked up on which can occur when you have read through your paper so many times already and it almost seems second nature to you and your committee members.

This of course comes at your own cost and can take a few more weeks to get done, but it is well worth the time and cost to ensure that when people read your work, that it looks as professional as possible. In many cases, your editor will work with you to word things more specifically. An editor will also ensure that they keep the essence of what you are sharing while cleaning it up so it will read well, especially when it comes to your quotes which they may want to clean up to fit proper grammar rules.

One thing that I experienced that was a little scary in my own work was that my editor got a little confused with culture-based education and place-based education and they wanted to change all of the wording to place-based education. My editor thought that it would read better and felt that it would make it a universal concept within the paper. After a few revisions, I had to explain the difference between the two: culture-based education is essentially place-based education but it includes the culture, language, and values of a particular culture so it takes place-based education to a higher level. Without my input, my paper could have totally been transformed into something that I did not want. In stating this, I caution you to be very involved in the editing of your paper and to make sure that you stand strong on what you think would be best for your study.

Some universities may also require you to bind your dissertation. To fulfill this requirement, you will need a publishing company that does leather binding and to send them a PDF copy of your dissertation. Make sure to ask them to use special, thicker book paper and they bind so that it lasts long in the library. I know that although this is an older practice, many universities like to house published dissertations in their library for other students to review and for the university to showcase the work of their students.

I myself ordered about 10 copies of my binded dissertation and shared one with each of my committee members as parting gifts. I also gave one to my mother, I kept one for myself, and I put one in the university library. Although this was an extra cost, I like having that one copy on my own bookshelf to really serve as a reminder of the hard work that I put into the program. A personal copy is a souvenir of achievement.

LESSONS LEARNED

1. When we defend our disertation it does not mean that we will pass and move forward to binding.
2. Be prepared! Make good use of different tools like PowerPoint notes and/or index cards to make sure you don't forget any important details.
3. There will be many more corrections and a process by which we finalize our dissertation before we are done.
5. Be prepared and know your study before your defense. Your committee will challenge your understanding with new questions that will get you to reflect on the implications of your study.

Jamie Dela Cruz

Critical Writing: Stories as Phenomena

Chapter 11 - Reflection: The Dissertation is Just the Beginning

As you near the end of the dissertation process and look toward graduation, you should understand that this is only the beginning of a lifetime of research ahead of you. Yes, I know that what I just expressed herein is likely difficult for you to believe. However, there is so much more ahead of you. Hopefully completing a great dissertation will set you up for a great career and a worthy study that will be able to take you places upon completing the dissertation and receiving your doctoral degree.

Many doctoral students, including myself, are always looking for ways to move forward in their careers. As we look for future employment, we try to "beef up" our resumes or professional vitae in order to showcase the breadth of our work experience and contributions to the field of academia. With this understanding our dissertation can be one of those pieces we we can use to quickly showcase our talents as a researcher and can serve as a basis of the work quality that we are able to produce.

For many of you I would like to wish you the best of luck at writing publications while you are in your program of study, participating in postdoctoral pieces and publishing them, or even on finding a spinoff of your dissertation or thesis pieces to explore further. These kinds of pieces will serve you well if you want to continue down the path of being a researcher and to find work at the university level that would be required of you.

It was about a year after I finished my dissertation when I really thought about starting more research and publishing with the support of my colleagues and especially from the dean of Argosy University. It was a hard road for me to decide on what I really wanted to do because I knew what was ahead of me if I wanted to start writing again. My first experience writing a lengthy piece was not the most positive one and I did not know if I wanted to start that process all over again.

My journey started with keeping in touch with my dissertational chair who was still teaching classes at Argosy University. Dr. Parrtington always welcomed me to drop in and talk about my research design. Through discussing with many of my colleagues who were doctoral students about the phenomenological methodology, many have decided to take on the challenge of doing a qualitative study, with some even deciding to use phenomenology as their main focus. By participating in discussions about my dissertation and the accompanying experiences with colleagues, I was able to keep many of my ideas fresh in my head as I started to write this book. You may never know where life may take you and may never know the direction you're headed. So always take notes on your good ideas because you never know where you may end up.

In seeing how these simple strategies were helping my friends succeed, I began jotting down notes and started writing some of the learned lessons from my experience to possibly help upcoming and budding researchers in the field, as well. As I began to write more, the writing process became a little more intriguing for me. Writing just felt like a natural medium to tell my story so that I could help more than the students at my school to learn from experiences in using phenomenological studies. I truly have enjoyed the process of learning through this style of data collection and find myself using these same strategies in my elementary school classroom with my students.

My post-doctoral work has led me to continue my passion for helping others and to share my knowledge with all of you. For me, I have enjoyed a more passive style of writing compared to the style used in my dissertation, which was more academic in nature where you have to be very technical. I have found this new experience of writing more satisfying and more relaxing. I hope that all of you learn from my experiences and begin to publish books of your own. Although I have taken time to recover from my dreadful experience, reflecting upon the dissertational process has really revealed to me on how I still love to learn. I am finding an internal need for continued professional growth.

As lifelong learners, doctoral candidates seem to have an innate sense to continue learning, no matter where they go. There is so much to learn about the world around us. Therefore, I hope that you continue to grow academically, professionally, and personally. I also hope that my stories have inspired you to believe that anything can be possible. Just as important, all we need to do is believe in ourselves and understand that although the road ahead may not be smooth riding, our hard work is well worth the extra effort.

For me, I have been very lucky to have had many doors opened as a result of having my doctorate. Although there are no guarantees in life, but I do feel that an education can pave many new avenues to success. For all of you who are reading this book, I encourage you to spread your wings and share your research with others just as I have done the same. Whether it be through a formal presentation at a local or national conference or just sharing your research with other colleagues, every step goes a long way. By taking on these kinds of challenges, you also allow others who may not have access to your study to learn about your research to expand their understanding as well. In doing so, many new opportunities can arise for further research and possible new publications. In taking these steps, you will be able to write your own story. New paths for success will allow you to find new ways to expand your horizons and find new opportunities for further learning. I hope that in the future I will be able to see more publications with the use of phenomenological research models as researchers are making a great name for themselves in their respective fields. Then the wealth of knowledge can be shared with those who want to learn from not only our experiences but from those who participated in studies.

I would like to point out that publishing, presenting at conferences, or even continued research will not be the only way to continue your education. However, I am simply planting a seed in your mind of possible ways to expand your research. Like many other students, I was a little hesitant when I was first asked to apply toward presenting at a local research conference. As I look back on my first experience presenting at a research conference, it was a little nerve-racking because I did not know what to expect. I was also nervous about how my research would stack up to the other studies at the conference.

For those of you who are willing to get out there to share your research there are a few steps in making this all possible. The first step would be to find out about local conferences that fit your research. For me since I did a program evaluation of a Native Hawaiian grant, I chose to apply to a Hawaiian research organization and a evaluation conference based in Hawaii. I did think about going to a bigger conference like the Pan Pacific but never made it there.

After you decide on what conference you would like to present at, you would also need to think about how you would like to share your research. In most conferences, researchers are asked to share their findings or strategies in a small group breakout, poster presentation, or a major speaker who speaks to a large group. As you think about what method may work best for you, you would need to break your study down and summarize it into a format that the organization will have ready for you. Generally they would ask for the implications of your work, your methodology and the major findings that you wish to share. If they find that noteworthy they will select your piece to be a part of their conference. Best of luck to you as you will meet tons of other people to network with who may be in your same field of study and expertise.

All of those worries were put to rest as soon as I got my feet wet and started meeting other professionals who were interested in learning about my topic. Since my dissertation, I am glad to report that I have presented at two state-level educational conferences, which include the Hawaii Educational Research Association (HERA) Conference in Hawaii and the Hawaii Pacific Evaluators Association (HPEA) conference also in Hawaii. Presenting has allowed me to share my research with other professionals in the field of education and evaluation. As I continue to grow as a researcher, I am now a grant evaluator for local grants in the State of Hawaii. I am still a classroom teacher at a local elementary school.

As a recent graduate, there is always self-doubt on how people will perceive your study because we are naturally very critical of ourselves. For me, I was able to present the findings of the research conducted in my dissertation as I did some post-doctoral studies soon after completing my program. For me it was like sharing my exact study or a spin off of my dissertation. Luckily, I only had to condense my own study and I worked with the Pacific American Foundation (the company who I did my research with) to come up with a topic that they would allow me to share.

Presenting at the conference was the biggest step that I have made with my study. Since our grant that I worked on was part of the Native Hawaiian Education Association (NHEA) it was great to share my style of evaluation with others who received funding from the same money source. In the past evaluation was not an important component of this process, which was why there was there was only a limited amount of literature that existed in my field before my study. Hopefully through presenting at these conferences, other researchers were able to take what they could from my study in formulating their own strategies for evaluating Hawaiian culture-based grants. From there, we can all work together in creating new models for a better future for Native Hawaiian students and grants so that many more students can benefit from new styles of evaluation and move the field of evaluation forward so that future generations can enjoy the fruits of continued work.

Although I do understand that I will have to one day leave the classroom to expand my horizons as a professional in the field of education, I really feel that the classroom has been a grounding place for me to start learning. Humble beginnings as an elementary school teacher and doctorate student have allowed me to understand my research methodology so much more clearly. These humble beginnings in working with young children have also allowed me to understand how clear communication can affect those around you. In our career we are constantly reminded that when we are not able to communicate our expectations and our content well our students are in a state of chaos and misunderstanding. Through my study and being able to help guide my participants to explain their experiences, it has helped me to become a better communicator in my every day living as well as in my work.

In looking back at my growth since my dissertation, I feel that the phenomenological study has really allowed me to grow as an individual and as a professional in my field. For me I feel that through my study I have become a better communicator in what I do and have such an appreciation for each person that I meet. It has also taught be the value of perseverance in everything that I do in doing through an arduous process of writing a dissertation. I am forever grateful for having the experiences that I have had throughout my educational career and would not change anything about it.

The Truth

The dissertational process has really been a learning process for me. I learned about myself and showed that when I really put my mind to something, I can achieve anything that I want to. The important part is that we need to take it one step at a time. Although the educational and dissertation process has been a challenge, I hope that you have learned about ways to make your own life easier through reading my experiences as you enter the process. The dissertation is the stepping stone by which we as researchers will build a career upon. The dissertation should not be the final piece of research that capstones our careers, however.

As I look back and reflect on my experiences as a doctoral candidate,

I feel that I am now in a good place for a more unbiased reflection, which has helped me to evaluate my past and future goals as well. I feel that I am also able to more clearly evaluate my experiences as a doctoral student. Through having discussions with doctoral students and sharing my experiences to prepare them for the adventure ahead as they start their dissertation phase, I have been able to better understand my experiences as a student myself. Through this informal learning, reflections about the experiences in my educational career have helped me to better understand and appreciate the ways in which this experience in itself has impacted my life for the better, even though the experience at the time was not particularly pleasant while it was happening.

In a sense, my phenomenological study has come full circle for me. I have not only used the methodology in my academic life but also in my professional and personal life. Through doing case studies and program evaluations especially with culture-based education, it has helped me to become not only respectful of who I work with, but come into situations more open minded in the way that I approach people and the way that I speak with them. Phenomenological methods can go very far in helping us make sense of our lives as adults and to reinforce the importance of self-reflection and personal growth. Through the work that I have done, I feel that I have a greater appreciation for others and what they can bring to the table and ways that I can learn from each person I meet. In doing so, we can be more aware of ourselves and our behaviors and become better people.

I am forever thankful to all of those who pushed me to use a qualitative study using phenomenology because it has really helped to shape the person I am today; through learning about this methodology, I have learned so much about others and the different ways of thinking that occurs for people. Most importantly, I have learned so much about myself as a person. In addition, this learning theory has helped me to better appreciate the different views that people have and ways that I can be more culturally sensitive to others.

I have learned that as human beings, learning never stops. As humans, we have an innate curiosity to learn about different things. Although we may never learn about everything the world has to offer, we try our best to learn as much as possible. Although we may make mistakes in the process of learning, we continue to learn not to let those speed bumps get in our way. Also, we learn that those bumps will make us stronger and more determined when we get back up to start again.

As you can see, the dissertation can be the beginning of a lifetime of continued growth and research. When we do get to this phase, we demonstrate that we have the drive and need for continuous self-improvement. Thus, confidence in your abilities is important and I encourage you to share your talents with the world.

Upon graduating, I could never have imagined that I would be in the position that I am now. Writing a book a year ago would have seemed crazy to me. Moreover, I was definitely not thinking about presenting my research at a conference. As life has taken its course, here I am almost two years later with a different perspective on my research and a new attitude for continued success in my professional life.

I did not know where life was going to take me after my dissertation and I allowed different opportunities to come to me. I chose to participate in activities and events that I felt most comfortable starting out with. Through continued encouragement from those around me, I am surprised at the amount of risks that I have taken since the publication of my dissertation. In looking back, I could not have asked for a better support group for my career and the paths that have enabled tracking. I am very lucky to be supported so much by loved ones and supporters and without them I would not be where I am today. In understanding this, life upon graduating can hold a little of the unknown. By surrounding yourself with people who are truly there in your best interest, they will encourage you to be your best. I have been very fortunate to have been surrounded by such great people. I hope that you will find the same kind of people in your life. It really helps to take the next step if others believe in you and what you do.

Always remember that when you become a doctor, you are now considered an expert in the field of your study. Through having done a significant study and contributed to your field, you are able to speak to your colleagues about your contributions and how it can affect the target groups that you have studied. During our academic career as a doctoral student, I was always told that what we doctoral students do does not matter because many of my professors believed that without conducting your own study and creating new findings that adds to the current literature that already exists, you are only restating what has already been done by others. At Argosy, doctoral students were not permitted to use the word "I" in writing assignments. Now, as I write this book, it is so hard to write from a different perspective given that I was conditioned to write using a certain perspective while doing all of my graduate work. Take time to appreciate your status as a new doctor and always be willing to share your wisdom with others who want to learn from you.

Although your dissertation will never fully define who you are and what you have accomplished, it will go a long way in setting you up for further success. If you do a great job, employers will take notice of your work and will request your help and insight to improve their organizations. In most cases, employers will request copies of your written work that may not be publicly available—like your dissertation—if they do not subscribe to a dissertation database like Proquest. They may have access to publicly written journals that you may have written for during your time of study or if they would like to know more, they generally request those from you. Through these written pieces, employers can see firsthand the quality of your work and what to expect if you were working in their organization. If they find your work to be valuable and helpful to helping move their organization forward, it will help you to take on new positions in your field. To me this is an additional resource that employers can look at that sometimes goes beyond your interview and your recommendations from your references.

Hopefully, through years of hard work on your dissertation, people will notice your efforts. Your years of hard work will also hopefully help you to start a great career for you. Like me, if you have a chance to present your research, try it out and allow people to learn from your research as well. Presenting your research publicly also establishes you as a field expert, worth consulting with. Doing so will allow you to get your research to others and for a broader market to be exposed to a different type of research that may have not seen before, which may spark an interest for employment or further research. In looking back at my experiences, I think that it is best to keep an open mind when you complete your dissertation.

Many doors can open for you only if you are willing to share your research with others so that they too can learn from your knowledge and experience. I am not saying that you have to follow in my footsteps and present at conferences, to mentor other students at your university, or to even share your research with others but am suggesting that these types of activities can really help open new doors for success. These successes can come in the form of job offers, new opportunities for continued research in your field, or just the self-satisfaction of helping others to learn from the experiences of the participants in your study or even your own experiences. You have a lot to offer. I would not sell yourself short when you have accomplished very much. Take time to celebrate your accomplishments and, help others who may want to learn from your study or your experiences.

Like a philanthropist who opens new doors of success for those who need the extra support through providing monetary support, you will be able to open new doors of success to people who need a little more support academically and emotionally. Through your knowledge, you can help many others who may need that extra support or encouragement. You need to be selfless in your actions. Through your words and experiences, you will learn that you can help inspire others to be the best that they can be.

If you expect great things for yourself, great things will happen to you. I wish you the best of success in whatever path you choose after finishing your doctoral degree. Through your hard work, I hope that you will be offered many great opportunities for continued professional success. Take time to celebrate your efforts and be confident in sharing your knowledge with those around you.

As I leave you, I highly suggest that you share your talents with the world. I hope that through these stories of how my dissertation helped me in my career, it has inspired you in your own journey of where life may take you. Spread you wings and take many risks. May your research act as a spring board for future success in your life.

Lessons Learned

1. The dissertation is not the end of your educational journey.
2. Get your research out there and share your knowledge with others. Be proud of your work and you will not regret it!
3. Network with others in your field of research and it will open

many new doors for future employment and reaching your career goals.
4. This is the beginning of your new life as a doctor!

Jamie Dela Cruz

Critical Writing: Stories as Phenomena

Parting Statement

Foremost, I would like to thank you for spending the time to read this book and for learning about my journey through my dissertation process. I hope that you have appreciated the stories that I have told and that you were able to step into my shoes to really understand the challenges that are ahead of you I hope that the stories herein have inspired you to begin your journey as a prominent phenomenological researcher. And I hope that you were able to take away some value that will help you become a better researcher and, most of all, a more conscious individual. I encourage you to be the best that you can. Whether it be a formal study like a dissertation or an informal independent study for your own personal growth, may this book help you in whatever capacity you may need.

This is not to say that the way I set up my study is the only way to conduct a successful research study, but can be used as a basis by which you can better understand how to set up a study of your own I hope that you have gained more insight into doing a phenomenological dissertation from the mistakes that I have made and the lessons that I have passed on to you. It is with hope that you will take the lessons learned to make yourself a more effective researcher who will go on to make great contributions to your field of study. My hat goes off to you in your journey of ongoing learning through continued research. There is so much to learn about the phenomenological methodology and I hope that this book puts things into more of a realistic point of view and allows you to better understand things to focus on as you start your own journey. Phenomenology really is a great style of methodology and I would like to praise you for taking on the challenge of trying to use it. Many people shy away from this particular style of methodology because it requires performing intricate analysis. However, it does offer you a chance to challenge your skills as a researcher in synthesizing all of the qualitative data. It really is an exhilarating experience in learning about others and the world around us.

It is important to understand that each person understands the world in a different way. It is not to say that one person's view is better than another's, but the goal is to become more aware of the world around us through the experiences of others. In doing so, we are able to learn more about ourselves and ways to improve our actions in our daily lives.

Sometimes, the everyday reading of a doctoral student can really bog you down with technicalities without giving you a down to earth appeal to it. I hope that this book has helped you understand areas that could be problematic and also the areas to really appreciate. Remember take time to enjoy yourself and to really hone down on great foundational skills which will help get you off to a great study. I wish you the best of luck in your dissertational journey. Remember, the dissertation is only the beginning of a great career for you. It is the means to an end, but not the end to the means.

For some people, the dissertation is the final, formal writing piece that they will ever publish within their lifetime. Upon graduating, I definitely considered my dissertation to be my final research project and thought that I would continue to work as an elementary school teacher while considering to search for a university-level teaching job once I was up for a different challenge. I was completely happy with the career track I was on and wanted to take some time to enjoy all of my hard work. Upon the completion of my dissertation and graduating, I thought that I was thoroughly done with school, too. I was so frustrated with the dissertation process that I truly never wanted to see an academic paper ever again.

After graduation, I was unable to become accustomed to having less structure in my life without all of the extra school work that was customary for me to complete each day. With this extra time, I was constantly reminded of the opportunity to publish a book as the dean of my college continued to support my efforts and encouraged me that it was important to share your knowledge and story to help those students who may be in the same position as myself during this arduous process. During this time, I was not that interested in authoring a book because I had just completed my dissertation; my dissertation in itself caused me enough grief toward publishing it therefore, I did not even consider starting such a large project at that time

It was about a year after I finished my dissertation when I really thought about starting more research and publishing with the support of my colleagues and especially from the dean of Argosy University. It was a hard road to come to a decision on what I really wanted to do because I knew what was ahead of me if I wanted to start writing again. My first experience writing a lengthy body of work was not the most positive one and I did not know if I wanted to start that process all over again.

The challenge of writing a book proved to be very daunting. I decided to start with mentoring some of my friends who were just starting in their dissertations. At first Argosy University would call me in to assist and speak in support groups for doctoral students to make sure that they could speak about problems that they were encountering in their dissertation process and for them to have someone there who could give them advice on how to overcome these obstacles. As time went on, students who were in the program would call me for help as they were in different portions of the program, to help them get through different parts of their dissertation like the IRB, setting up their literature review, or even for the final review and binding of their work. For those I have mentored, I liked how my advice seemed to help each of them throughout their process. Some of them did not want to believe everything I communicated to them and I did my best to explain what I knew to them. My mentees needed to encounter the process themselves and find out that what I expressed was all to true. As my friends and I look back at it now, we still laugh because they remember me explaining that same process to them while they didn't really want to hear the reality of the situation.

Jamie Dela Cruz

About the Author

Dr. Jamie Dela Cruz currently resides on the island of Oahu in the state of Hawaii. He enjoys the "simple life" and continues to keep himself active in the field of education by taking on new roles in different schools around the state. He is a well-rounded individual who enjoys spending lots of time outdoors with friends and time with his family. Having spent most of his professional years as an elementary educator, he enjoys finding time for himself and finding a good balance of work life and play.

Jamie graduated from Argosy University with a Doctorate in Organizational Leadership and also has a Master's in Elementary Education. He has been an elementary school teacher for more than ten years, serving the Honolulu District in Honolulu, Hawaii. Jamie has taught and created professional development courses at the University of Phoenix for the university's college of education program. Aside from a successful career in academia, Jamie has served as an external consultant for Honda Educational Learning Partners helping them run logistics to enhance learning goals and strategic planning, and completes grant writing projects and evaluations for companies based in Hawaii.

To learn more about Jamie and follow his literary career, visit www.savantbooksandpublications.com/delacruzjamie.

Jamie Dela Cruz

Index

A

academ(ia, ic, ally) 5, 37-8, 54, 70, 94, 103, 107, 111, 155, 157-8, 163, 165, 168, 173, 177
adage 124-5
advi(ce, se, sor) 3-5, 10, 39, 42, 90, 94, 112, 133-5, 137, 140, 142, 174
aloha 1-2, 13-4
analy(sis, ze) 4, 19, 23, 31-4, 36-8, 40-2, 48, 58, 60-1, 83, 115, 117-9, 123, 125-6, 139, 132-4, 136, 139, 142, 144, 172
APA 151

B

behav(e, ior) 22, 27, 33, 45, 163
belief 2, 20, 22
bias 2, 31, 39, 54, 21, 115, 117, 163
Buckingham (Gertrude Tooley) 125

C

capstone 87, 162
categor(ize, y) 32, 41, 122, 125, 140
checklist 71, 80, 84-5

colle (ague, ge, iate) 2, 6, 9, 93-4, 111, 131, 151, 158, 165, 173-4, 177

Columbine High School 3

committee, doctoral 34–37, 41, 49, 81, 88, 91, 93-4, 103, 110, 118–120, 131–143, 145–153

communicat(e, ion, or) 4-5, 13, 19, 26, 33, 45, 51, 61, 138, 148, 161-72, 176

consent 48, 71, 80, 93

coursework 101, 103, 142

cultur(al, e) 2, 13-5, 18-20, 37, 47, 50, 61, 76, 117-8, 121, 124, 151, 152, 161, 163-4

D

data(base) 3, 14, 16, 18–9, 22, 24, 27, 31-43, 46, 48, 52, 54, 57, 60, 64, 67, 70, 77, 82, 93, 110, 116–7, 120, 122–3, 125–6, 129, 133–4, 137, 139–40, 142, 144, 157, 168, 172

debrief(e, ing) 15, 151

defense 92, 132, 137, 146–8, 150–1, 153

discrepancies 117

discuss(ion) 17, 26, 28, 34, 36-7, 46, 52-6, 68, 66, 69, 73-9, 83, 106-7, 146-51, 156, 163

dissertation 2–5, 9–10, 12, 20, 31, 33–38, 41, 47, 50, 64, 69, 73, 79–82, 87–97, 102–112, 116, 119–120, 123–125, 131–147, 149–153, 155–157, 160, 162–168, 171–174

doctor(al, ate) 1-2, 6–7, 9–10, 88, 92, 95, 98, 103-4, 106, 108–12, 120, 132, 134, 143, 155–8, 160–3, 165-6, 168, 172, 174

document(ation) 15, 20, 103, 128

E

edit(or) 87, 151–2
educat(e, ion, or) 2, 6, 14, 36, 90, 122, 151–2, 158–61, 163, 177
empathy 21, 54, 69
employ(ee, er) 174
evaluat(e, tion, or) 10,14, 22–4, 27, 29, 32, 46, 57, 116, 119, 127, 132-3, 140, 142, 149-50, 159-171, 160, 163
experience 3–4, 9–10, 12, 14–8, 20–8, 33–9, 42, 45–52, 54–7, 59–66 68–71, 73–5, 78, 81, 101, 112, 116–21, 124, 126–7, 129, 133, 135–40, 156-7, 159, 162–3, 167–8, 180

F

feedback 5, 94, 128
format 70, 76, 151, 160

G

graduat(e, ing) 92, 103, 112, 123, 16, 164-166, 173
guid(ance, e) 7, 16, 27-8, 43, 50, 56, 65-6, 68-9, 75, 79-81,116, 119, 132, 134–7, 139-40, 150, 162, 110-111, 177

H

habits 107
Hawaii(an) 1–2, 6, 10, 13–4, 48-9, 105, 117, 121, 159–61, 177
HERA 160
heuristic 2
HPEA 160

I

incentiv(e, izing) 87–9, 91–2, 96–8
inspir(ation, e) 12, 14, 33, 36, 91, 94, 97, 135, 158, 166, 171
internal(ize) 7, 37, 42, 87, 91-2, 94, 129, 157
interview(ing) 2–5, 13–4, 18, 21–8, 31–4, 35, 45, 47-7, 59-68, 70-1, 73–8, 80-1, 83-4, 93, 115-122, 124, 125, 128-129, 134, 139, 147, 766
IRB 4 7, 91–2, 97, 104, 110, 145, 174

J

journal 71, 115, 127

K

kinesthetic 45

L

language 2, 37, 37, 75, 129, 152
literature 4, 82, 104, 109–10, 131, 145–6, 161, 166, 174

M

methodology 3, 18, 51, 67, 69, 92, 104, 124, 131, 136–7, 142, 147, 156, 160–1, 163–4, 172
milestone 91–2
misrepresent(ation) 33, 51, 119
MLA 141
model 22, 59–60, 84, 138, 158, 161
music 1

N

NHEA 161
notations 115
notebook 75, 80, 115

O

organiz(e, ing) 12, 31-2, 35, 40, 42, 81, 104, 108, 122-3, 126, 140
outl(iers, y) 32, 82

P

Pacific American Foundation 29, 152
phenomen (a, ological, ology) 2-4, 6-7, 9-28, 37-41, 45-8, 50-52, 56-7, 62, 64-5, 67-8, 71-5, 92, 117, 122, 124-5, 128, 135, 142, 156-8, 162-4, 171-172, 183
PowerPoint 147, 153
practice 13, 20, 28, 43, 107, 148, 152
preconception 42, 47, 56, 83
predisposition 27
prepar(ation, e) 21, 25-6, 64-8, 70, 73-4, 77-80, 92, 126, 144, 150, 153, 156, 158, 161, 171
presentation 24, 41, 117, 138, 143, 147-50, 158-9
Proquest 166
prospectus 91

Q

qualit(ative, y) 2–3, 24, 31, 42, 68, 70, 81, 84, 93, 102, 108, 115, 122, 125–6, 132, 138, 147, 156, 164, 166, 172
quantit(ative, y) 4, 81

R

reflect(ion) 5, 15, 18, 47, 50, 55, 83, 97, 129, 133, 135, 138, 145, 150, 153, 155, 157, 162-3

require(ment) 7, 14, 25, 45, 52, 70, 89, 101, 108, 115, 152, 156, 172

research(er) 1-3-5-7, 11–3, 15, 17-9, 22-8, 33, 38, 45, 47, 50-2, 54, 56-7, 59–61, 63, 65–71, 74-5, 77, 79–84, 104-5, 108, 111, 115-9, 123–4, 125–9, 132, 134, 137–9, 141-3, 146–7, 149, 155–6, 158–162, 164–5, 167–8, 171–4

responsibility 4

review 4, 23, 33, 36–7, 39, 41, 45, 82–3, 87, 93, 104, 110, 117, 121–2, 126, 131, 146–7, 151–2, 174

S

showcase 152, 155

social(exchange theory) 18, 51, 53, 55, 101, 112

speculat(e, ion) 49

spinoff 156

stor(ies, y, yteller, ytelling incl "talking story") 1-4, 7, 9, 11, 13-5, 17-22, 25, 27-9, 39, 42-3, 42-9, 52-3, 56, 65, 73, 75, 92, 101, 113, 121, 127, 134, 136, 139, 157-62, 171, 173, 184

suggest(ion) 54, 59-60, 66-7, 69, 71, 81, 96, 104-5, 108-10, 131-4, 138-41, 144, 147, 167-8

T

talk(ing story; see "storytelling")

theme, 15, 31–2, 34–5, 39–41, 55, 78, 117–8, 122–123, 124–5, 132, 134, 140

timeframe 64
tradition 18-20
transcription 15, 23, 31–4, 36, 41, 60, 83,
traum(a, atic) 5, 93
trust 22, 34, 52–3, 139
truth 6, 38 51, 65, 70, 81, 94, 105, 124, 141, 162

U-V

valid(ate, ity) 15, 33-4, 39, 47, 50, 52, 61, 66, 70, 115, 120, 123, 125
view(point) 19, 22, 33, 42-3, 50, 75-6, 121, 133, 164, 172

W

writ(e, en) 1-2, 7, 9-10, 19-20, 31-2, 36-8, 41, 45, 47-9, 71, 81, 83, 89, 91, 92-3, 97 103, 115, 118, 121, 125, 132, 134, 136, 139, 143, 149, 151, 155-8, 162, 164, 166, 173-4, 177, 185

Y

YMCA 132–3

Jamie Dela Cruz

If you enjoyed *CRITICAL WRITING: STORIES AS PHENOMENA*, consider these other fine books from Savant Books and Publications:

Essay, Essay, Essay by Yasuo Kobachi
Aloha from Coffee Island by Walter Miyanari
Footprints, Smiles and Little White Lies by Daniel S. Janik
The Illustrated Middle Earth by Daniel S. Janik
Last and Final Harvest by Daniel S. Janik
A Whale's Tale by Daniel S. Janik
Tropic of California by R. Page Kaufman
Tropic of California (the companion music CD) by R. Page Kaufman
The Village Curtain by Tony Tame
Dare to Love in Oz by William Maltese
The Interzone by Tatsuyuki Kobayashi
Today I Am a Man by Larry Rodness
The Bahrain Conspiracy by Bentley Gates
Called Home by Gloria Schumann
Kanaka Blues by Mike Farris
First Breath edited by Z. M. Oliver
Poor Rich by Jean Blasiar
The Jumper Chronicles by W. C. Peever
William Maltese's Flicker by William Maltese
My Unborn Child by Orest Stocco
Last Song of the Whales by Four Arrows
Perilous Panacea by Ronald Klueh
Falling but Fulfilled by Zachary M. Oliver
Mythical Voyage by Robin Ymer
Hello, Norma Jean by Sue Dolleris
Richer by Jean Blasiar
Manifest Intent by Mike Farris
Charlie No Face by David B. Seaburn
Number One Bestseller by Brian Morley
My Two Wives and Three Husbands by S. Stanley Gordon
In Dire Straits by Jim Currie
Wretched Land by Mila Komarnisky
Chan Kim by Ilan Herman
Who's Killing All the Lawyers? by A. G. Hayes
Ammon's Horn by G. Amati
Wavelengths edited by Zachary M. Oliver
Almost Paradise by Laurie Hanan
Communion by Jean Blasiar and Jonathan Marcantoni
The Oil Man by Leon Puissegur
Random Views of Asia from the Mid-Pacific by William E. Sharp
The Isla Vista Crucible by Reilly Ridgell
Blood Money by Scott Mastro
In the Himalayan Nights by Anoop Chandola
On My Behalf by Helen Doan
Traveler's Rest by Jonathan Marcantoni

Critical Writing: Stories as Phenomena

Keys in the River by Tendai Mwanaka
Chimney Bluffs by David B. Seaburn
The Loons by Sue Dolleris
Light Surfer by David Allan Williams
The Judas List by A. G. Hayes
Path of the Templar—Book 2 of The Jumper Chronicles by W. C. Peever
The Desperate Cycle by Tony Tame
Shutterbug by Buz Sawyer
Blessed are the Peacekeepers by Tom Donnelly and Mike Munger
The Bellwether Messages edited by D. S. Janik
The Turtle Dances by Daniel S. Janik
The Lazarus Conspiracies by Richard Rose
Purple Haze by George B. Hudson
Imminent Danger by A. G. Hayes
Lullaby Moon (CD) by Malia Elliott of Leon & Malia
Volutions edited by Suzanne Langford
In the Eyes of the Son by Hans Brinckmann
The Hanging of Dr. Hanson by Bentley Gates
Flight of Destiny by Francis Powell
Elaine of Corbenic by Tima Z. Newman
Ballerina Birdies by Marina Yamamoto
More More Time by David B. Seabird
Crazy Like Me by Erin Lee
Cleopatra Unconquered by Helen R. Davis
Valedictory by Daniel Scott
The Chemical Factor by A. G. Hayes
Quantum Death by A. G. Hayes and Raymond Gaynor
Big Heaven by Charlotte Hebert
Captain Riddle's Treasure by GV Rama Rao
All Things Await by Seth Clabough
Tsunami Libido by Cate Burns
Finding Kate by A. G. Hayes
The Adventures of Purple Head, Buddha Monkey and Sticky Feet by Erik and Forest Bracht
In the Shadows of My Mind by Andrew Massie
The Gumshoe by Richard Rose
In Search of Somatic Therapy by Setsuko Tsuchiya
Cereus by Z. Roux
The Solar Triangle by A. G. Hayes
Shadow and Light edited by Helen R. Davis
A Real Daughter by Lynne McKelvey
StoryTeller by Nicholas Bylotas
Bo Henry at Three Forks by Daniel Bradford
Kindred edited by Gary "Doc" Krinberg
Cleopatra Victorious by Helen R. Davis
Navel of the Sea by Elizabeth McKague
Entwined edited by Gary "Doc" Krinberg

Coming Soon

Jamie Dela Cruz

Crowned Rose of York by Carolina Casas
Short Beach: Memento Mori by Kenneth M. Kapp

Savant Books and Publications
http://www.savantbooksandpublications.com

Critical Writing: Stories as Phenomena

and from our *avant garde* imprint, Aignos Publishing:

The Dark Side of Sunshine by Paul Guzzo
Happy that it's Not True by Carlos Aleman
Cazadores de Libros Perdidos by German William Cabasssa Barber [Spanish]
The Desert and the City by Derek Bickerton
The Overnight Family Man by Paul Guzzo
There is No Cholera in Zimbabwe by Zachary M. Oliver
John Doe by Buz Sawyers
The Piano Tuner's Wife by Jean Yamasaki Toyama
Nuno by Carlos Aleman
An Aura of Greatness by Brendan P. Burns
Polonio Pass by Doc Krinberg
Iwana by Alvaro Leiva
University and King by Jeffrey Ryan Long
The Surreal Adventures of Dr. Mingus by Jesus Richard Felix Rodriguez
Letters by Buz Sawyers
In the Heart of the Country by Derek Bickerton
El Camino De Regreso by Maricruz Acuna [Spanish]
Diego in Two Places by Carlos Aleman
Prepositions by Jean Yamasaki Toyama
Deep Slumber of Dogs by Doc Krinberg
Saddam's Parrot by Jim Currie
Beneath Them by Natalie Roers
Chang the Magic Cat by A. G. Hayes
Illegal by E. M. Duesel
Island Wildlife: Exiles, Expats and Exotic Others by Robert Friedman
The Winter Spider by Doc Krinberg
The Princess in My Head by J. G. Matheny

Coming Soon:
Comic Crusaders by Richard Rose
I'll Remember by Clif Mc Crady

Aignos Publishing | an imprint of Savant Books and Publications
http://www.savantbooksandpublications.com

www.ingramcontent.com/pod-product-compliance
Lightning Source LLC
Chambersburg PA
CBHW061308110426
42742CB00012BA/2101